COPPER LODGE LIBRARY

EXPLORING INSECTS
WITH UNCLE PAUL

EDITED AND INTRODUCTION BY
Stephanie B. Meter

MULTIMEDIA

Exploring Insects with Uncle Paul (Copper Lodge Library)
© 2021 Classical Conversations® MultiMedia. All rights reserved.

Published by Classical Conversations, Inc.
255 Air Tool Drive
Southern Pines, NC 28387

CLASSICALCONVERSATIONS.COM
CLASSICALCONVERSATIONSBOOKS.COM

Cover design by Classical Conversations.
The cover artwork and illustrations were collected from a variety of illustrators.

This Copper Lodge Library edition is an abridged replication of the text of the first edition of *The Story-Book of Science*, originally published by The Century Company, New York, NY, 1917 and *Fabre's Book of Insects*, originally published by Dodd, Mead, and Company, New York, NY, 1921. Illustrations have been added specifically for the Copper Lodge Library edition. Slight changes in punctuation and/or spelling as well as parenthetical definitions have been included to improve readability.

Printed in the United States of America

All rights reserved. No part of this publication may be reproduced, stored in a retrieval system, or transmitted in any form by any means, electronic, mechanical, photocopy, recording, or otherwise, without prior permission of the author, except as provided by USA copyright law.

ISBN: 978-1-951571-22-1

ACKNOWLEDGMENTS

Thanks to. . .

Leigh Bortins for her passion for celebrating God's creation and for inspiring others to echo in celebration.

Jennifer Courtney for beautifully casting the vision for these projects through her love of reading, families, and wonder.

Karin Carpenter for her heart for clarity, excellence, and hospitality as she edited this book.

Sarah McElroy and Kathi James for mining the internet for just the right images and for making this book beautiful.

Leslie Hubbard for her gift of research and searching out hidden things, and for always helping me untangle things with such grace.

Lisa Bailey for breathing life into the entire Scribblers Curriculum in a way that makes me excited to have children one day.

TABLE OF CONTENTS

Introduction 7
How to Use This Book..11
How to Savor This Book...13
WEEK ONE
    The Six..25
    The Fairy Tale and The True Story......................................29
WEEK TWO
    The Building of the City...33
WEEK THREE
    The Cows..37
WEEK FOUR
    The Sheepfold 41
WEEK FIVE
    The Wily Dervish 47
WEEK SIX
    A Numerous Family 51
WEEK SEVEN
    The Old Pear-Tree 57
    The Age of Trees 61
WEEK EIGHT
    The Length of Animal Life 65
WEEK NINE
    The Kettle...69
    Metals 73
WEEK TEN
    Metal Plating..77
    Gold and Iron 81
WEEK ELEVEN
    The Fleece 85
    Flax and Hemp 89

WEEK TWELVE
   Cotton 93
WEEK THIRTEEN
   Butterflies 99
WEEK FOURTEEN
   The Big Eaters 103
WEEK FIFTEEN
   Silk 109
WEEK SIXTEEN
   The Metamorphosis 113
WEEK SEVENTEEN
   Spiders 117
WEEK EIGHTEEN
   The Epeira's Bridge 121
WEEK NINETEEN
   The Spider's Web 125
WEEK TWENTY
   The Chase 129
WEEK TWENTY-ONE
   Venomous Insects 133
WEEK TWENTY-TWO
   Venom 139
WEEK TWENTY-THREE
   The Viper and the Scorpion 143
WEEK TWENTY-FOUR
   The Sacred Beetle 147
Works Cited 152
Further Reading 153

INTRODUCTION

> This is my Father's world,
> And to my listening ears
> All nature sings, and round me rings
> The music of the spheres.
> This is my Father's world:
> I rest me in the thought
> Of rocks and trees, of skies and seas—
> His hand the wonders wrought.
> MALTBI D. BABCOCK
(1858-1901)

God's handiwork is so worthy of celebration. Together as a family, go outside and marvel at the world, from the smallest nearby earthworm to the vastness of space and the stars. Nothing knits hearts closer like encountering something together. Individually, the star-studded sky is breathtaking; a wiggly earthworm is a marvel. However, this celebration of creation can be more than a time of discovery, but a time of building sweet relationships in your family.

In addition to going out into nature, your family can pick up this book and read about creatures you might not be able to observe in your area. Both outside and in your reading, marvel at the strange, unique, detailed, and varied nature of God's creation. Your knowledge will cause you to echo in celebration of our Creator. As you read and explore, keep your eyes wide for how creation demonstrates that "all nature sings."

"Compared with truth, fiction is but a pitiful trifle; for the former is the work of God, the latter the dream of man." So Uncle Paul tells his niece and nephews when they ask him for a real story, not a fairytale.

Children love fairy tales. They love things that surprise them or seem mysterious. Fairy tales are a time-honored and worthy way to discover truths about our world. Fairy tales teach us about good and evil, consequences, bravery, grief, and countless other truths that can be applied to reality. How delightful is also is to discover that the "real world" can be as surprising, mysterious, wise, and wonderful as a fairytale! The natural world overflows with beauty, goodness, and truth at which to wonder. Science is not a textbook subject; it is a riot of excitement happening in our own backyards! Even better, it is a riot of excitement to be discovered together as a family.

The benefits of reading aloud cannot be overstated. Not only does reading aloud create an atmosphere of closeness and discovery, it helps develop a child's vocabulary. In fun stories about ants and aphids, children will hear terms they might not encounter otherwise. Through context and conversations, their minds will develop a basic knowledge of scientific ideas. As they continue to interact with the world, these ideas will recur and blossom into curiosity and critical thinking. Hearing stories out loud also makes it easier for them to notice rhetorical devices like rhyming, repetition, and parallelism.

Exploring Insects introduces science as something to be experienced at home, though conversations and stories rather than textbooks and diagrams alone. Uncle Paul delights his niece and nephews with tales of real creatures living among them. He is also an excellent role model for the homeschooling parent, as he is known for having "books of all kinds." Sometimes it is so easy to collect literature books that we forget to develop the other categories of our home libraries. As we read aloud books on all subjects, the world will come into sharper focus for our children and awaken in them a thirst for exploration. Uncle Paul also models a joy for detours! (A chapter on metal plating? In a book about insects?!) Families should be encouraged not to fear when one investigation gives way to curiosity about other things.

While *Exploring Insects* is a delightful book, it ought to be only a starting place for scientific discoveries at home! Read a story, then go outside and see it for yourselves. Find some ants and watch them work. Find some leaves, on a tree and on the ground. Touch bark. Smell the rain. Marvel at a bird's nest. Imagine what a bunny is thinking right now. Remember how different seasons feel on your skin, look to your eyes. Hear the wind.

"The world will never starve for want of wonders," G. K. Chesterton wrote. "but only for want of wonder."

We hope this Uncle Paul reader will fill you and your children with wonder!

HOW TO USE THIS BOOK

Classical Conversations® has created the Scribblers At-Home program for families of children ages four to eight (although all of the resources and activities can be enjoyed by students of all ages, even adults). The Scribblers resources are designed to mix read-alouds and hands-on activities to prepare families for a lifetime of learning. Scribblers to Scribes is designed to inspire confidence in you, the homeschooling parent, and teach you the classical method. Under your tutelage, your little "scribblers" will become scribes! Sow seeds of the fruit you are eager to harvest. This fruit is not just knowing scientific names and the origins of Latin but also the fruit of curiosity about the natural world and an understanding of allusions. Reading together and noticing echoes will help your children learn to listen for references and allusions. When they are little, you can introduce your children to specific allusions while teaching them to be attuned to these references for life.

Develop the habit of asking "Is this like anything else we've heard? How is this a new reflection or an echo of something old?"

This Scribblers reader is designed to be read about once a week. The Stories of Rome series is designed to be read once a week, and the Echoes books are designed to be read two to three times a week. Families can choose from any of the readers. Families who choose to read all of them will find that they have short selections to read every day of the week. The Uncle Paul's Science Stories prepares families for a lifetime of celebrating discoveries in the natural world. The Stories of Rome series prepares families for a study of history and debate and encourages families to look at the virtuous and not so virtuous actions of ancient rulers. The Echoes series prepares families for a lifetime enjoyment of stories which will allow them to learn from the choices of others.

"It is the glory of God to conceal a thing: but the honour of kings is to search out a matter." Proverbs 25:2

Embrace your inheritance as kings and queens, and go on a treasure hunt for the marvels of creation!

HOW TO SAVOR
THIS BOOK

As you share this book with your family, here are some tools that can help you dig deeper and enjoy the stories more fully.

FIVE CORE HABITS OF GRAMMAR

The "Five Core Habits" are skills that our littlest learners hone most naturally. Children love to know the names of things, notice details, memorize *everything*, sing, play games, and tell others all about it! Practicing these habits helps children to grow in their appreciation of the world and their ability to make discoveries and connections. While the Core Habits are most accessible to young learners, people of all ages can benefit from these basics in exploration.

NAMING

Naming is one of the first "games" that children play! Children love to know and share the names of people, places, and things. For young learners, questions like "Who is in this story?" and "What plants or animals are in this story?" can be an engaging interaction with the tale. For older children, questions about particular objects or new terms might be fun to explore. While naming seems simple, this Core Habit develops the ability to think in categories, to get both more general and more specific, and to understand how the world fits together. A conversation that names a bug can easily become a conversation about an insect or a plant-louse (also called an "aphid"). Conversations about a red-billed seagull can expand to a conversation about seagulls, or birds, or "oviparous" (egg-laying) animals. These naming conversations help children not only to learn new terminology, but also to understand the way terms and categories interact.

Example using "The Cows"

Who are the human characters? What are they like? How do you imagine they look? *Claire is almost twelve and is gentle, obedient, and enjoys knitting. Jules is nine and loves to ask questions, although he also has a temper sometimes. Emile is the youngest, is often messy, and likes to play with his toys, Uncle Paul is a grownup who loves to read and tell his niece and nephews about the world.*

What is an ant? What is an insect? *An ant is a small insect that lives in a large colony and is very industrious. An insect is a bug that has a three-part body, six legs, and an exoskeleton.*

What is "milk"? *For humans, milk is what female mammals produce to feed their offspring. For the ants, "milk" is the sugary sap that drips from the tubes of the plant lice as the lice drink the sap from the elder bush.*

What is a plant louse, according to Uncle Paul? *The plant lice function like cows for the ants!*

How to Take This Outside

Find some ants! Notice their parts. What do we call an ant's home?

Can you find any "plant lice" (also called aphids)? What kind of plants do you find them on?

Attending

Young children are often better than adults at attending to a story's surface details. This is a beautiful skill, since in great literature, surface details often contribute to deep symbolism. Help children also take note of patterns like the number of days or repeated phrases.

HOW TO SAVOR THIS BOOK

Encourage them to engage all five senses—and their imaginations!—when attending to a tale.

Example using "The Cows"
Five Senses
What does a bee sound like?
What would a tiny drop of milk sound like?
What does milk taste like?
What would a bush of white flowers smell like?
What do you think the "plant lice" look like?
What does it feel like to have a full belly? What would it feel like to have an ant tickle you with his antennae?

Setting
Where does the story take place? *The characters' names are French, so the story probably takes place in France. "The Cows" story takes place in the garden.*

In what kind of habitat or biome does the story take place? (Wet? Dry? Shady? In the dirt? In a tree?) How is the animal or insect suited for its habitat? *The garden is probably watered and weeded. The plant lice are on the underside of the leaves of an elder bush, where it is shady and probably cooler.*

What time of year might it take place? (Think about the bush with white flowers!) *This story probably takes place in the spring.*

Does the story change locations, moving from one place to another?

Characters
Who are the human characters in this story? *Uncle Paul, Claire, Jules, Emile*

Who are the non-human characters in the story? *The plant lice, the ants*

Plot
How does the story start? *The children remember Uncle Paul's mention of "cows" for ants and go to find him and get him to tell them more.*

What do the characters desire? *They want to learn more about plant lice!*

Pick a character and discuss the character's actions. What did he/she/it do first? Next? Next? *Emile wakes up and remembers "the cows." He enlists Jules's help in getting Uncle Paul to tell them more. They find Uncle Paul. Uncle Paul takes them to the garden and they look under the leaves of the elder bush...*

How does the story end? *They have learned about plant lice and how ants take news back to their colonies. Emile and Jules continue looking for plant lice in the garden.*

Conflict

Is there a problem in the beginning, or a struggle to get what someone wants? How do the characters deal with this? Did they make good choices? Were there any different ways to get what they wanted? *In this story, the human characters want to hear from Uncle Paul about the plant lice. They do not have to struggle very hard to get what they want here!*

What do the ants need from the plant-lice? How do they get what they need? *The ants want "milk" from the plant lice, and they have to tickle the lice to get what they want.*

Theme

What did you find interesting or weird in this story? *We learned that although it looked at first like the ants were being gluttonous, they were actually taking food back to share with their colonies.*

Does the story remind you of anything you've heard somewhere else? *Maybe the story reminds you of the ants in* A Bug's Life. *Maybe the ravenous appetites of the ants make you think about* The Very Hungry Caterpillar.

What can you celebrate about God's creation and His design? *The Bible has lots to say about serving your community, about not being selfish, and about using gentleness to get what you want or need!*

Memorizing

As you probably already know, memorizing comes very naturally to young ones! Children learn to speak their native languages through listening and memorizing. Everything is newer to children, and they thrive on repetition. Rereading favorite stories will inevitably lead to memorization after a while.

How to Take This Outside:

Practice naming and remembering things like the names of the seasons, the parts of a flower, the parts of a tree, the parts of an insect.

Say aloud things you notice and make connections to things you've seen before.

Connect present explorations to experiences you've had in the past. "Look, the leaves are changing color! Remember how green they used to be? Remember how shiny they were when we came outside during the rain?"

Expressing

Young children have very active bodies that are intimately connected to their minds. There are several ways for them to express what they have learned from your reading.

Narration: Give children a few minutes to tell back the story they have just heard. Putting it into their own words encourages creativity and thoughtful processing.

Acting: Allow children to act out the story throughout the week. Go outside and find the appropriate setting, real props, and maybe even an audience of backyard animals to perform for!

Drawing: Children often attend better to read-alouds if their hands are busy. They can illustrate the stories and poems while you read, then go outside and find specimens to sketch in a nature journal.

Copywork: Have the children use their best handwriting to copy a sentence or paragraph about their nature sketch. This journal can develop into a beautiful keepsake of scientific play!

STORYTELLING

Children love to tell stories. They can retell the stories you are reading to them, imagine sequels, or re-imagine the tales altogether! Allow them to be creative, changing the setting or plot or characters. Many will likely be inspired to document their own scientific discovery stories, sometimes backed by slightly (or extremely) dubious scientific evidence. Let their imaginations soar. There will be other times and places to respect the laws of reality.

FIVE COMMON TOPICS OF DIALECTIC

The Five Common Topics can help children—and anyone else—explore in more depth. Asking Common Topic questions is an excellent springboard into understanding a story, a problem, an experience, a choice, a person, or just about anything else. Build a foundation for understanding through definition questions. Orient a problem or story using comparison to connect familiar dots and uncover questions worth pursuing. Gain clarity and compassion by examining the circumstances in a story. Explore cause and effect and "what if?" by asking relationship questions. Look to others for wisdom or expertise by asking "who has something to say about this?" Although usually seen in this order, the Five Common Topics can be wielded well in any order and to whatever extent serves you best. They are tools, not a checklist!

DEFINITION

Definition questions ask what a thing is, what its parts are, what groups it belongs to, and what distinguishes it from others of the same group. Definition questions might include naming characters and locations, listing as many characteristics of the characters and locations as possible, or defining unfamiliar terms.

Examples using "The Cows"

Who or what are the characters? What are their characteristics? What groups do they belong to? What makes them different from other people or things in their same group? *Claire is almost twelve and is gentle, obedient, and enjoys knitting. She is like other almost-twelve-year-old girls, but she is also unlike them because she lives somewhere else, has brothers named Jules and Emile, and has a different temperament and hobbies than some other girls. Jules is nine and loves to ask questions, although he also has a temper sometimes. Emile is the youngest, is often messy, and likes to play with his toys. Uncle Paul is a grownup who loves to read and tell his niece and nephews about the world.*

What is an insect? What are its parts? What is an exoskeleton? *An insect is a bug that has a three-part body, six legs, and an exoskeleton. An exoskeleton is a hard external covering.*

What is a "glutton"? *A glutton is someone or something that overeats, especially as a habit.*

How to Take This Outside

Name the things you observe: trees, clouds, dirt, bugs, flowers, rocks, puddles…

What are their parts? What are the purposes of their parts?

What makes them different from other things of their same groups?

Comparison

Children naturally compare things when they are assessing or trying to understand them. We can casually compare any two things, people, places, or situations in our conversations. If we want to be very systematic about it, we can compare two things by listing what they both have, what they both are, and what they both do. As we list similarities, we will inevitably discover interesting differences as well.

Examples using "The Cows"

How are the plant lice similar to and different from "real" cows? *They are similar to cows because they provide a liquid food to other animals, can "be milked," graze together with others of their kind. They are different from cows in that they are tiny, they don't have udders, and they are a different species!*

How are Claire, Jules, and Emile similar to and different from each other? *They are all curious human children and they are all French. Claire is a girl while Jules and Emile are boys. Their temperaments and hobbies make them very different from each other.*

How are ants similar to and different from the plant lice? *Both are small, insects, live in the garden, need food to survive, live in groups. They are different types of insects. The ants rely on the plant lice.*

How are ants similar to and different from people? *The ants look outside of themselves for food, live in groups, work together, seem industrious. Ants and people are very different sizes, communicate with each other through different means, and have different minds. Ants are driven by instincts whereas people are rational and can make moral choices.*

How to Take This Outside

Compare the leaves on different types of trees.

Compare a flower stem and a tree trunk.

Compare the dirt at the bottom of a puddle to the dirt in a garden.

Compare the sun and the moon.

Compare fog and rain.

Compare an ant and a grasshopper.

Compare different types of birds.

The possibilities are absolutely endless!

CIRCUMSTANCE

Circumstance questions deal with the context and events surrounding a story or situation. What else was going on at the same time in the same place? What about in a different place? Has anything like this happened before? Under what circumstances could something like this happen again? What actions or decisions were possible under these circumstances? Impossible? Unpacking a story's circumstances helps us to empathize with others and to attempt to make the wisest decisions we can.

> Examples using "The Cows"
> What time of day does the story take place? *In the morning*
> What season does the story take place? Why do you think that? *Possibly in the spring because the elder bush is flowering.*
> Why are the children staying with Uncle Paul? *Uncle Paul loves to talk with and share knowledge with children, so he has asked his brother—the children's father—to let the children stay with him for a while.*

How to Take This Outside:

What is the weather like today? What is the weather like where your grandparents live? What is the weather like in a country in another hemisphere?

Do you remember another time when the weather was like this? Do you think the weather will be like this again?

Would it be possible to build a sandcastle in your backyard? Would it be possible to build a snowman in your backyard today? Would it be a good day to go swimming or play in the hose?

Think about the habitats of different bugs or animals. What kind of "home" do they live in? Do they make a home, or do they live out in the open? How are their bodies designed to work with their surroundings?

Relationship

Relationship questions deal with cause and effect, and "what if" questions. What happened before? What happened after? What were the causes/effects? What would have happened if "X" had been different?

While these questions sometimes seem like a roundabout way to retell a story, they can also lead to noticing new connections between causes and effects. Was X really an effect of Y? Did something even further back cause X? What were all the effects of Y?

Examples using "The Cows"

What happens first? *The children wake up and decide they need to hear the story of the ants' cows.*

What happens next? *They go to Uncle Paul and ask him, and he says he will show them rather than tell them.*

What happens next? *They go outside and see the bush with the white flowers. They see the ants swarming up and down the bush's trunk. Some of the ants have full-looking bellies.*

What would have happened if Uncle Paul had said no? How would the story be different if Uncle Paul had just told the children about the plant-lice instead of showing them? *The children would have been disappointed if Uncle Paul had refused to tell them more. They might have been less likely to ask him questions in the future. If Uncle Paul had just told the children about the plant lice, they wouldn't have asked the same questions or been able to see the relationship firsthand. They might not have realized the plant lice were in their very own garden.*

What do they see when they look very closely at the ants? *They see that they have very full bellies and seem "on a mission."*

What happens when the ants tickle the plant-lice? *The plant lice allow a litle bit of "milk" to drip down the tubs on their backs.*

How to Take This Outside:

What caused the puddles? What caused the dirt to crack?

What caused the leaves to change color?

What made the weather warm/cold today?

What effect will the rain have on the dirt? On your garden? On the bird's nest? On the anthill?

What would the rabbit do if you walked closer to it?

What happened to the bird on the birdfeeder when a bigger bird came along?

What happens to a flower after it is picked? Does putting it into a vase of water make a difference as opposed to leaving it lying on the table?

Testimony

Who has something to say about this? Is he or she trustworthy?

Examples using "The Cows"

What authority does Uncle Paul have to speak about ants? *Uncle Paul reads lots of scientific books and enjoys experimenting and exploring for himself. He has done research and had personal experiences that allow him to speak about ants.*

What laws of math or science do you see in the story? *Everyone has to eat! Plant lice's digestions work differently than humans'. Gravity pulls on the drops of "milk." The ants' bellies swell when they're full.*

How to Take This Outside

Where can you go to find the names of different plants, animals, bugs, and weather?

What does the Bible say about plants, animals, and weather? Are there any Bible stories that come to mind?

Use these Core Habits and Common Topics as tools to help you learn and have fun, not as a checklist to be completed! We hope that *Exploring Insects* will fill you and your children with wonder at all the wonders!

Illustration by unknown artist in *The Quiver: An Illustrated Magazine for Sunday and General Reading* (London: Cassell & Company, 1891).

Week One:
The Six

One evening, at twilight, they were assembled in a group, all six of them. Uncle Paul was reading in a large book. He always reads to rest himself from his labors, finding that after work nothing refreshes so much as communion with a book that teaches us the best that others have done, said, and thought. He has in his room, well arranged on pine shelves, books of all kinds. There are large and small ones, with and without pictures, bound and unbound, and even gilt-edged ones. When he shuts himself up in his room it takes something very serious to divert him from his reading. And so they say that Uncle Paul knows any number of stories. He investigates, he observes for himself. When he walks in his garden he is seen now and then to stop before the hive, around which the bees are humming, or under the elder bush, from which the little flowers fall softly, like flakes of snow; sometimes he stoops to the ground for a better view of a little crawling insect, or a blade of grass just pushing into view.

What does he see! What does he observe! Who knows! They say, however, that there comes to his beaming face a holy joy, as if he had just found himself face to face with some secret of the wonders of God. It makes us feel better when we hear stories that he tells at these moments; we feel better, and furthermore we learn a number of things that some day may be very useful to us.

Uncle Paul is an excellent, God-fearing man, obliging to every one, and "as good as bread." The village has the greatest esteem for him, so much so that they call him Maître [Master] Paul, on account of his learning, which is at the service of all.

To help him in his field work—for I must tell you that Uncle Paul knows how to handle a plow as well as a book, and cultivates his little estate with success—he has Jacques, the old husband of old Ambroisine. Mother Ambroisine has the care of the house, Jacques looks after the animals and fields. They are better than two servants; they are two friends in whom Uncle Paul has every confidence. They saw Paul born and have been in the house a long, long time. How often has Jacques made whistles from the bark of a willow to console little Paul when he was unhappy! How many times Ambroisine, to encourage him to go to school without crying, has put a hard-boiled new-laid egg in his lunch basket!

So Paul has a great veneration for his father's two old servants. His house is their house. You should see, too, how Jacques and Mother Ambroisine love their master! For him, they would do anything. Uncle Paul has no family, he is alone; yet he is never happier than when with children, children who chatter, who ask this, that, and the other, with the adorable ingenuousness of an awakening mind. He has prevailed upon his brother to let his children spend a part of the year with their uncle. There are three: Emile, Jules, and Claire.

Claire is the oldest. When the first cherries come she will be twelve years old. Little Claire is industrious, obedient, gentle, a little timid, but not in the least vain. She knits stockings, hems handkerchiefs, studies her lessons, without thinking of what dress she shall wear Sunday. When her uncle, or Mother Ambroisine, who is almost a mother to her, tells her to do a certain thing, she does it at once, even with pleasure, happy in being able to render some little service. It is a very good quality.

Jules is two years younger. He is a rather thin little body, lively, all fire and flame. When he is preoccupied about something, he does not sleep. He has an insatiable appetite for knowledge. Everything interests and takes possession of him. An ant drawing a straw, a sparrow chirping on the roof, are sufficient to engross his attention. He then turns to his uncle with his interminable questions: Why is this? Why is that? His uncle has great faith in this curiosity, which, properly guided, may lead to good results. But there is one thing about Jules that his uncle does not like. As we must be honest, we will own that Jules has a little fault which would become a grave one if not guarded against: he has a temper. If he is opposed he cries, gets angry, makes big eyes, and spitefully throws away his cap.

But it is like the boiling over of milk soup: a trifle will calm him. Uncle Paul hopes to be able to bring him round by gentle reprimands, for Jules has a good heart.

Emile, the youngest of the three, is a complete madcap; his age permits it. If any one gets a face smeared with berries, a bump on the forehead, or a thorn in the finger, it is sure to be he. As much as Jules and Claire enjoy a new book, he enjoys a visit to his box of playthings. And what has he not in the way of playthings? Now it is a spinning-top that makes a loud hum, then blue and red lead soldiers, a Noah's Ark with all sorts of animals, a trumpet which his uncle has forbidden him to blow because it makes too much noise, then—But he is the only one that knows what there is in that famous box. Let us say at once, before we forget it, Emile is already asking questions of his uncle. His attention is awakening. He begins to understand that in this world a good top is not everything. If one of these days he should forget his box of playthings for a story, no one would be surprised.

"A pile of books in a field, under the sun." Illustration by unknown artist in *Lights and Shadows of European History* by S. G. Goodrich (Boston: Bradbury, Soden, & Co., 1844).

Week One:
THE FAIRY TALE AND THE TRUE STORY

THE six of them were gathered together. Uncle Paul was reading in a big book, Jacques braiding a wicker basket, Mother Ambroisine plying her distaff, Claire marking linen with red thread, Emile and Jules playing with the Noah's Ark. And when they had lined up the horse after the camel, the dog after the horse, then the sheep, donkey, ox, lion, elephant, bear, gazelle, and a great many others,—when they had them all arranged in a long procession leading to the ark, Emile and Jules, tired of playing, said to Mother Ambroisine: "Tell us a story, Mother Ambroisine—one that will amuse us."

And with the simplicity of old age Mother Ambroisine spoke as follows, at the same time twirling her spindle:

"Once upon a time a grasshopper went to the fair with an ant. The river was all frozen. Then the grasshopper gave a jump and landed on the other side of the ice, but the ant could not do this; and it said to the grasshopper: 'Take me on your shoulders; I weigh so little.' But the grasshopper said: 'Do as I do; give a spring, and jump.' The ant gave a spring, but slipped and broke its leg.

"Ice, ice, the strong should be kind; but you are wicked to have broken the ant's leg—poor little leg.

"Then the ice said: 'The sun is stronger than I, and it melts me.'

"Sun, sun, the strong should be kind; but you are wicked, to melt the ice; and you, ice, to have broken the ant's leg—poor little leg.

"Then the sun said: 'The clouds are stronger than I; they hide me.'

"Clouds, clouds, the strong should be kind; but you are wicked, to hide the sun; you, sun, to melt the ice; and you, ice, to have broken the ant's leg—poor little leg.

"Then the clouds said: 'The wind is stronger than we; it drives us away.'

"Wind, wind, the strong should be kind; but you are wicked, to drive away the clouds; you, clouds, to hide the sun; you, sun, to melt the ice; and you, ice, to have broken the ant's leg—poor little leg.

"Then the wind said: 'The walls are stronger than I; they stop me.'

"Walls, walls, the strong should be kind; but you are wicked, to stop the wind; you, wind, to drive away the clouds; you, clouds, to hide the sun; you, sun, to melt the ice; and you, ice, to have broken the ant's leg—poor little leg.

"Then the walls said: 'The rat is stronger than we; it bores holes through us.'

"Rat, rat, the strong—"

"But it is all the same thing, over and over again, Mother Ambroisine," exclaimed Jules impatiently.

"Not quite, my child. After the rat comes the cat that eats the rat, then the broom that strikes the cat, then the fire that burns the broom, then the water that puts out the fire, then the ox that quenches his thirst with the water, then the fly that stings the ox, then the swallow that snaps up the fly, then the snare that catches the swallow, then—"

"And does it go on very long like that?" asked Emile.

"As long as you please," replied Mother Ambroisine, "for however strong one may be, there are always others stronger still."

"Really, Mother Ambroisine," said Emile, "that story tires me."

"Then listen to this one: Once upon a time there lived a woodchopper and his wife, and they were very poor. They had seven children, the youngest so very, very small that a wooden shoe answered for its bed."

"I know that story," again interposed Emile. "The seven children are going to get lost in the woods. Little Hop-o'-my-Thumb marks the way at first with white pebbles, then with bread crumbs. Birds eat

THE FAIRY TALE AND THE TRUE STORY

the crumbs. The children get lost. Hop-o'-my-Thumb, from the top of a tree, sees a light in the distance. They run to it: rat-tat-tat! It is the dwelling of an ogre!"

"There is no truth in that," declared Jules, "nor in Puss-in-Boots, nor Cinderella, nor Bluebeard. They are fairy tales, not true stories. For my part, I want stories that are really and truly so."

At the words, true stories, Uncle Paul raised his head and closed his big book. A fine opportunity offered for turning the conversation to more useful and interesting subjects than Mother Ambroisine's old tales.

"I approve of your wanting true stories," said he. "You will find in them at the same time the marvelous, which pleases so much at your age, and also the useful, with which even at your age you must concern yourselves, in preparation for after life. Believe me, a true story is much more interesting than a tale in which ogres smell fresh blood and fairies change pumpkins into carriages and lizards into lackeys. And could it be otherwise? Compared with truth, fiction is but a pitiful trifle; for the former is the work of God, the latter the dream of man. Mother Ambroisine could not interest you with the ant that broke its leg in trying to cross the ice. Shall I be more fortunate? Who wants to hear a true story of real ants?"

"I! I!" cried Emile, Jules, and Claire all together.

"Ants harvesting buffalo-grass." Illustration by unknown artist in *Nature's Craftsmen: Popular Studies of Ants and Other Insects* by Henry C. McCook (New York and London: Harper and Brothers. 1907).

Week Two:
The Building of the City

"They are noble workers," began Uncle Paul, "Many a time, when the morning sun begins to warm up, I have taken pleasure in observing the activity that reigns around their little mounds of earth, each with its summit pierced by a hole for exit and entrance.

"There are some that come from the bottom of this hole. Others follow them, and still more, on and on. They carry between their teeth a tiny grain of earth, an enormous weight for them. Arrived at the top of the mound, they let their burden fall, and it rolls over the slope, and they immediately descend again into their well. They do not play on the way, or stop with their companions to rest a while. Oh, no! The work is urgent, and they have so much to do Each one arrives, serious, with its grain of earth, deposits it, and descends in search of another. What are they so busy about?

"They are building a subterranean town, with streets, squares, dormitories, storehouses; they are hollowing out a dwelling-place for themselves and their family. At a depth where rain cannot penetrate, they dig the earth and pierce it with galleries, which lengthen into long communicating streets, subdivided into short ones, crossing one another here and there, sometimes ascending, sometimes descending, and opening into large halls. These immense works are executed grain by grain, drawn by strength of the jaws. If any one could see that black army of miners at work under the ground, he would be filled with astonishment.

"They are there by the thousands, scratching, biting, drawing, pulling, in the deepest darkness. What patience! What efforts! And when the grain of sand has at last given way, how they go off, head held high and proud, carrying it triumphantly above! I have seen ants, whose heads tottered under the tremendous load, exhaust themselves in getting to the top of the mound. In jostling their companions, they seemed to say: See how I work! And nobody could blame them, for the pride of work is a noble pride. Little by little, at the gate of the town, that is to say at the edge of the hole, this little mound of earth is piled up, formed by excavated material from the city that is being built. The larger the mound, the larger the subterranean dwelling, it is plain.

"Hollowing out these galleries in the ground is not all; they must also prevent landslides, fortify weak places, uphold the vaults with pillars, make partitions. These miners are then seconded by carpenters. The first carry the earth out of the ant-hill, the second bring the building materials. What are these materials! They are pieces of timber-work, beams, and small joists, suitable for the edifice. A tiny little bit of straw is a solid beam for a ceiling, the stem of a dry leaf can become a strong column. The carpenters explore the neighboring forests, that is to say the tufts of grass, to choose their pieces.

"Good! see this covering of an oat-grain. It is very thin, dry, and solid. It will make an excellent plank for the partition they are constructing below. But it is heavy, enormously heavy. The ant that has made the discovery draws backward and makes itself rigid on its six feet. No success: the heavy mass does not move. It tries again, all its little body trembling with energy. The oat-husk just moves a tiny bit. The ant recognizes its powerlessness. It goes off. Will it abandon the piece? Oh, no! When one is an ant, one has the perseverance that commands success. Here it is coming back with two helpers. One seizes the oat in front, the others hitch themselves to the side, and behold! it rolls, it advances; it will get there. There are difficult steps, but the ants they meet along the route will give them a shoulder.

"They have succeeded, not without trouble. The oat is at the entrance to the underground city. Now things become complicated; the piece gets awry; leaning against the edge of the hole, it cannot enter. Helpers hasten up. Ten, twenty unite their efforts without success. Two or three of them, engineers perhaps, detach themselves from the band, and seek the cause of this insurmountable resistance. The difficulty is soon solved: they must put the piece with the point at the bottom. The oat is drawn back a little, so that one end overhangs the hole. One ant seizes this end while the others lift the end that is on the ground, and the piece, taming a somersault, falls into the well, but is prudently held on to by the carpenters clinging to the sides. You may perhaps think, my children, that the miners mounting with their grain of earth would stop from curiosity before this mechanical prodigy? Not at all, they have not time. They pass with their loads of excavated material, without a glance at the carpenters' work. In their ardor they are even bold enough to slide under the moving beams, at the risk of being crippled. Let them look out! That is their affair.

"One must eat when one works so hard. Nothing creates an appetite like violent exercise. Milkmaid ants go through the ranks; they have just milked the cows and are now distributing the milk to the workers."

Here Emile burst out laughing. "But that is not really and truly so!" said he to his uncle. "Milkmaid ants, cows, milk! It is a fairy tale like Mother Ambroisine's."

Emile was not the only one to be surprised at the peculiar expressions Uncle Paul had used. Mother Ambroisine no longer turned her spindle, Jacques did not plait his wickers, Jules and Claire stared with wide-open eyes. All thought it a jest.

"No, my dears," said Uncle Paul. "I am not jesting; no. I have not exchanged the truth for a fairy tale. It is true there are milkmaid ants and cows. But as that demands some explanation, we will put off the continuation of the story until tomorrow."

Emile drew Jules off into a comer, and said to him in confidence: "Uncle's true stories are very amusing, much more so than Mother

Ambroisine's tales. To hear the rest about those wonderful cows, I would willingly leave my Noah's Ark."

"Honey-ant workers obtaining honey from a honey-bearer." Illustration by unknown artist in *Nature's Craftsmen: Popular Studies of Ants and Other Insects* by Henry C. McCook (New York and London: Harper and Brothers. 1907).

Week Three:
The Cows

THE next day Emile, when only half awake, began to think of the ants' cows. "We must beg uncle," said he to Jules, "to tell us the rest of his story this morning."

No sooner said than done: they went to look for their uncle.

"Aha!" cried he upon hearing their request, "The ants' cows are interesting you. I will do better than tell you about them, I will show them to you. First of all call Claire."

Claire came in haste. Their uncle took them under the elder bush in the garden, and this is what they saw:

The bush is white with flowers. Bees, flies, beetles, butterflies, fly from one flower to another with a drowsy murmur. On the trunk of the elder, amongst the ridges of the bark, numbers of ants are crawling, some ascending, some descending. Those ascending are the more eager. They sometimes stop the others on the way and appear to consult them as to what is going on above. Being informed, they begin climbing again with even more ardor, proof that the news is good. Those descending go in a leisurely manner, with short steps. Willingly they halt to rest or to give advice to those who consult them. One can easily guess the cause of the difference in eagerness of those ascending and those descending. The descending ants have their stomachs swollen, heavy, deformed, so full are they; those ascending have their stomachs thin, folded up, crying hunger. You cannot mistake them:

the descending ants are coming back from a feast and, well fed, are returning home with the slowness that a heavy paunch demands; the ascending ants are running to the same feast and put into the assault of the bush the eagerness of an empty stomach.

"What do they find on the elder to fill their stomachs!" asked Jules. "Here are some that can hardly drag along. Oh, the gluttons!"

"Gluttons! no," Uncle Paul corrected him; "for they have a worthy motive for gorging themselves. There is above, on the elder, an immense number of the cows. The descending ants have just milked them, and it is in their paunch that they carry the milk for the common nourishment of the ant-hill colony. Let us look at the cows and the way of milking them. Don't expect, I warn you, herds like ours. One leaf serves them for pasturage."

Uncle Paul drew down to the children's level the top of a branch, and all looked at it attentively. Innumerable black velvety lice, immobile and so close together as to touch one another, cover the under side of the leaves and the still tender wood. With a sucker more delicate than a hair plunged into the bark, they fill themselves peacefully with the sap of the elder without changing their position. At the end of their back, they have two short and hollow hairs, two tubes from which, if you look attentively, you can see a little drop of sugary liquid escape from time to time. These black lice are called plant-lice. They are the ants' cows. The two tubes are the udders, and the liquor which drips from their extremity is the milk. In the midst of the herd, on the herd, even, when the cattle are too close together, the famished ants come and go from one louse to another, watching for the delicious little drop. The one who sees it runs, drink, enjoys it, and seems to say on raising its little head: Oh, how good, oh, how good it is! Then it goes on its way looking for another mouthful of milk. But plant-lice are stingy with their milk; they are not always disposed to let it run through their tubes. Then the ant, like a milkmaid ready to milk her cow, lavishes the most endearing caresses on the plant-louse. With its antennae, that is to say, with its little delicate flexible horns, it gently pats the stomach and tickles the milk-tubes. The ant nearly always succeeds. What cannot

"Ants collecting honeydew from an aphid herd." Illustration by unknown artist in *Nature's Craftsmen: Popular Studies of Ants and Other Insects* by Henry C. McCook (New York and London: Harper and Brothers. 1907).

gentleness accomplish! The plant-louse lets itself be conquered; a drop appears which is immediately licked up. Oh, how good, how good! As the little paunch is not full, the ant goes to other plant-lice trying the same caresses.

Uncle Paul let go of the branch, which sprang back into its natural position. Milkmaids, cattle, and pasture were at once at the top of the elder bush.

"That is wonderful, Uncle," cried Claire.

"Wonderful, my dear child. The elder is not the only bush that nourishes milk herds for the ants. Plant-lice can be found on many other forms of vegetation. Those on the rosebush and cabbage are green; on the elder, bean, poppy, nettle, willow, poplar, black; on the oak and thistle, a bronze color; on the oleander and nut, yellow. All have the two tubes from which oozes the sugary liquor; all vie with one another in feasting the ants."

Claire and her uncle went in-doors. Emile and Jules, enraptured by what they had just seen, began to look for lice on other plants. In less than an hour they had found four different kinds, all receiving visits of no disinterested sort from the ants.

"An emmet shepherdess carrying one of her aphid flock," illustration by unknown artist in *Nature's Craftsmen: Popular Studies of Ants and Other Insects* by Henry C. McCook (New York and London: Harper and Brothers. 1907).

Week Four:
THE SHEEPFOLD

IN the evening Uncle Paul resumed the story of the ants. At that hour Jacques was in the habit of going the round of the stables to see if the oxen were eating their fodder and if the well-fed lambs were sleeping peacefully beside their mothers. Under the pretense of giving the finishing touches to his wicker basket, Jacques stayed where he was. The real reason was that the ants' cows were on his mind. Uncle Paul related in detail what they had seen in the morning on the elder: how the plant-lice let the sugary drops ooze from their tubes, how the ants drank this delicious liquid and knew how, if necessary, to obtain it by caresses.

"What you are telling us, Master," said Jacques, "puts warmth into my old veins. I see once more how God takes care of His creatures. He gives the plant-louse to the ant as He gives the cow to man."

"Yes, my good Jacques," returned Uncle Paul,

"These things are done to increase our faith in Providence, whose all-seeing eye nothing can escape. To a thoughtful person, the beetle that drinks from the depths of a flower, the tuft of moss that receives the rain-drop on the burning tile, bear witness to the divine goodness.

"To return to my story. If our cows wandered at will in the country, if we were obliged to take troublesome journeys to go and milk them in distant pastures, uncertain whether we should find them or not, it would be hard work for us, and very often impossible. How do we manage them? We keep them close at hand, in enclosures and in stables. This also is sometimes done by the ants with the plant-lice. To avoid tiresome journeys, sometimes useless, they put their herds in a park. Not all have this admirable foresight, however. Besides, if they had, it would be impossible to construct a park large enough for such innumerable cattle and their pasturage. How, for example, could they enclose in walls the willow that we saw this morning with its population of black lice! It is necessary to have conditions that are not beyond the forces available. Given a tuft of grass whose base is covered with a few plant-lice, the park is practicable.

"Ants that have found a little herd plan how to build a sheepfold, a summer chalet, where the plant-lice can be enclosed, sheltered from the too bright rays of the sun. They too will stay at the chalet for some time, so as to have the cows within reach and to milk them at leisure. To this end, they begin by removing a little of the earth at the base of the tuft so as to uncover the upper part of the root. This exposed part forms a sort of natural frame on which the building can rest. Now grains of damp earth are piled up one by one and shaped into a large vault, which rests on the frame of the roots and surrounds the stem above the point occupied by the plant-lice. Openings are made for the service of the sheepfold. The chalet is finished. Its inmates enjoy cool and quiet, with an assured supply of provisions. What more is needed for happiness? The cows are there, very peaceful, at their rack, that is to say, fixed by their suckers to the bark. Without leaving home the ants can drink to satiety that sweet milk from the tubes.

"Let us say, then, that the sheepfold made of clay is a building of not much importance, raised with little expense and hastily. One could overturn it by blowing hard. Why lavish such pains on so temporary a shelter? Does the shepherd in the high mountains take more care of his hut of pine branches, which must serve him for one or two months?

"It is said that ants are not satisfied with enclosing small herds of plant-lice found at the base of a tuft of grass, but that they also bring into the sheepfold plant-lice encountered at a distance. They thus make a herd for themselves when they do not find one already made. This mark of great foresight would not surprise me; but I dare not certify it, never having had the chance to prove it myself. What I have seen with my own eyes is the sheepfold of the plant-lice. If Jules looks carefully he will find some this summer, when the days are warmest, at the base of various potted plants."

"You may be sure, Uncle," said Jules, "I shall look for them. I want to see those strange ants' chalets. You have not yet told us why ants gorge themselves so, when they have the good luck to find a herd of plant-lice. You said those descending the elder with their big stomachs were going to distribute the food in the ant-hill."

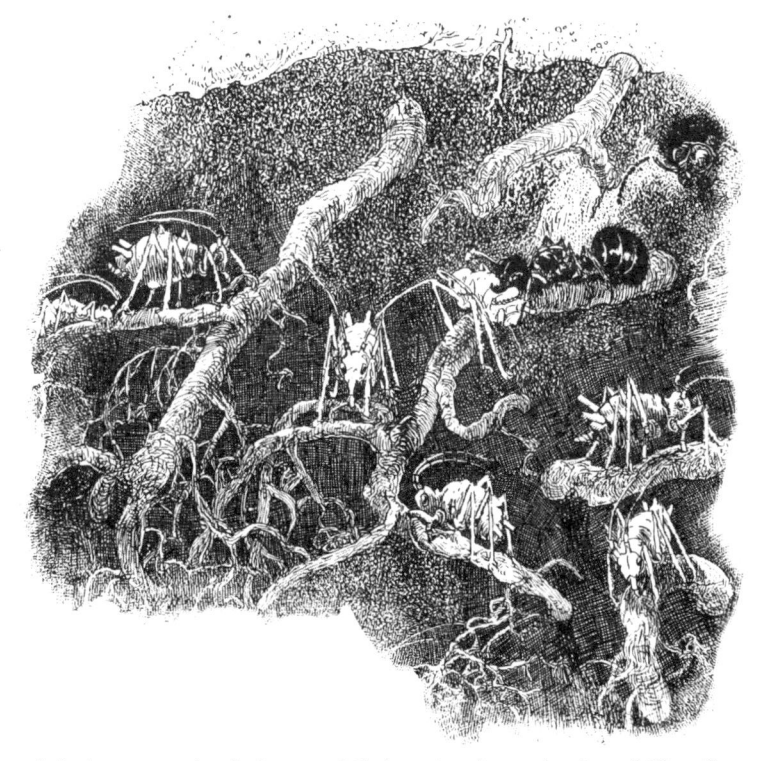

"A broken section of earth, showing aphids domesticated upon plants' roots." All ant illustrations in this story by unknown artist in *Nature's Craftsmen: Popular Studies of Ants and Other Insects* by Henry C. McCook (New York and London: Harper and Brothers. 1907).

"A foraging ant does not fail to regale itself on its own account if the occasion offers; and it is only fair. Before working for others must one not take care of one's own strength! But as soon as it has fed itself, it thinks of the other hungry ones. Among men, my child, it does not always happen so. There are people who, well fed themselves, think everybody else has dined. They are called egoists. God forbid your ever bearing that sorry name, of which the ant, paltry little creature, would be ashamed! As soon as it is satisfied, then, the ant remembers the hungry ones, and consequently fills the only vessel it has for carrying liquid food home; that is to say, its paunch.

"Now see it returning, with its swollen stomach. Oh! how it has stuffed so that others may eat! Miners, carpenters, and all the workers occupied in building the city await it so as to resume their work heartily, for pressing occupations do not permit them to go and seek the plant-lice themselves. It meets a carpenter, who for an instant drops his straw. The two ants meet mouth to mouth, as if to kiss. The milk-carrying ant disgorges a tiny little bit of the contents of its paunch, and the other one drinks the drop with avidity. Delicious! Oh! now how courageously it will work! The carpenter goes back to his straw again, the milk-carrier continues his delivery route. Another hungry one is met. Another kiss, another drop disgorged and passed from mouth to mouth. And so on with all the ants that present themselves, until the paunch is emptied. The milk-ant then departs to fill up its can again.

"Now, you can imagine that, to feed by the beakful a crowd of workers who cannot go themselves for victuals, one milk-ant is not enough; there must be a host of them. And then, under the ground, in the warm dormitories, there is another population of hungry ones. They are the young ants, the family, the hope of the city. I must tell you that ants, as well as other insects, hatch from an egg, like birds."

"One day," interposed Emile, "I lifted up a stone and saw a lot of little white grains that the ants hastened to carry away under the ground."

"Those white grains were eggs," said Uncle Paul, "which the ants had brought up from the bottom of their dwelling to expose them under the stone to the heat of the sun and facilitate their hatching. They hurried to descend again, when the stone was raised, so as to put them in a safe place, sheltered from danger.

"On coming out from the egg, the ant has not the form that you know. It is a little white worm, without feet, and quite powerless, not even able to move. There are in an ant-hill thousands of those little worms. Without stop or rest, the ants go from one to another, distributing a beakful, so that they begin to grow and change in one day into ants. I leave you to think how much they must work and how many plant-lice must be milked, merely to nurse the little ones that fill the dormitories."

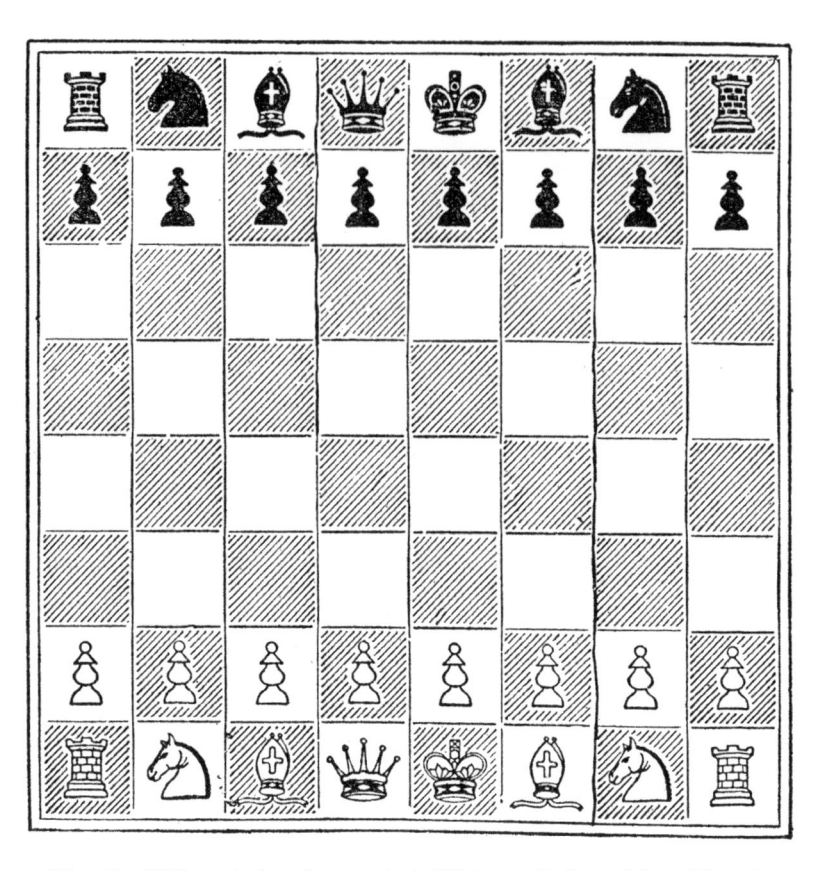

"Chess Board." Illustration by unknown artist in *Hill's Practical Reference Library Volume II* by L. Brent Vaughan (New York: Dixon, Hanson and Company, 1906).

Week Five:
The Wily Dervish

"THERE are ant-hills everywhere, large or small," observed Jules. "Even in the garden I could have counted a dozen. From some the ants are so numerous they blacken the road when they come out. It must take a great many plant-lice to nourish all that little colony."

"Numerous though they be," his uncle assured him, "They will never lack cows, as plant-lice are still more numerous. There are so many that they often seriously menace our harvests. The miserable louse declares war against us. To understand it, listen to this story:

"There was once a king of India who was much bored. To entertain him, a dervish invented the game of chess. You do not know this game. Well, on a board something like a checkerboard two adversaries range, in battle array, one white, the other black, pieces of different values: pawns, knights, bishops, castles, queen and king. The action begins. The pawns, simple foot-soldiers, are destined as always to receive the first of the glory on the battlefield. The king looks on at their extermination, guarded by his grandeur far from the fray. Now the cavalry charge, slashing with their swords right and left; even the bishops fight with hot-headed enthusiasm, and the ambulating castles go here and there, protecting the flanks of the army. Victory is decided. Of the blacks, the queen is a prisoner; the king has lost his castles; one knight and one bishop do wonderful deeds to procure his flight. They succumb. The king is checkmated. The game is lost.

"This clever game, image of war, pleased the bored king very much, and he asked the dervish what reward he desired for his invention.

"'Light of the faithful,' answered the inventor, 'a poor dervish is easily satisfied. You shall give me one grain of wheat for the first square of the chessboard, two for the second, four for the third, eight for the fourth, and you will double thus the number of grains, to the last square, which is the sixty-fourth. I shall be satisfied with that. My blue pigeons will have enough grain for some days.'

"'This man is a fool,' said the king to himself; 'he might have had great riches and he asks me for a few handfuls of wheat.' Then, turning to his minister:—'Count out ten purses of a thousand sequins for this man, and have a sack of wheat given him. He will have a hundred times the amount of grain he asks of me.'

"'Commander of the faithful,' answered the dervish, 'keep the purses of sequins, useless to my blue pigeons, and give me the wheat as I wish.'

"'Very well. Instead of one sack, you shall have a hundred.'

"'It is not enough, Sun of Justice.'

"'You shall have a thousand.'

"'Not enough, Terror of the unfaithful. The squares of my chessboard would not have their proper amount.'

"In the meantime the courtiers whispered among themselves, astonished at the singular pretensions of the dervish, who, in the contents of a thousand sacks, would not find his grain of wheat doubled sixty-four times. Out of patience, the king convoked the learned men to hold a meeting and calculate the grains of wheat demanded. The dervish smiled maliciously in his beard, and modestly moved aside while awaiting the end of the calculation.

"And behold, under the pen of the calculators, the figure grew larger and larger. The work finished, the head one rose.

"'Sublime Commander,' said he, 'arithmetic has decided. To satisfy the dervish's demand, there is not enough wheat in your granaries. There is not enough in the town, in the kingdom, or in the whole world. For the quantity of grain demanded, the whole earth, sea and continents together, would be covered with a continuous bed to the depth of a finger.'

"The king angrily bit his mustache and, unable to count out to him his grains of wheat, named the inventor of chess prime vizier. That is what the wily dervish wanted."

"Like the king, I should have fallen into the dervish's snare," said Jules. "I should have thought that doubling a grain sixty-four times would only give a few handfuls of wheat."

"Henceforth," returned Uncle Paul, "you will know that a number, even very small, when multiplied a number of times by the same figure, is like a snow-ball which grows in rolling, and soon becomes an enormous ball which all our efforts cannot move."

"Your dervish was very crafty," remarked Emile. "He modestly contented himself with one grain of wheat for his blue pigeons, on condition that they doubled the number on each square. Apparently, he asked next to nothing; in reality, he asked more than the king possessed. What is a dervish, Uncle?"

"In the religions of the East they call by that name those who renounce the world to give themselves up to prayer and contemplation."

"You say the king made him prime vizier. Is that a high office."

"Prime vizier means prime minister. The dervish then became the greatest dignitary of the State, after the king."

"I am no longer surprised that he refused the ten purses of a thousand sequins. He was waiting for something better. The ten purses, however, would make a good sum!"

"A sequin is a gold piece worth about twelve francs. At that rate, the king offered the dervish a sum of one hundred and twenty thousand francs, besides the sacks of wheat."

"And the dervish preferred the grain sixty-four times doubled."

"In comparison what was offered him was nothing."

"And the plant-lice?" asked Jules.

"The story of the dervish is bringing us to that directly," his uncle assured him.

"Woolly aphid is a plant lice. Eggs are attached to twigs during the winter. In the spring soft-bodied, wingless female aphids appear and give birth to young aphids. They suck the juices from leaves or twigs." Illustration by unknown artist in *Standard Cyclopedia of Horticulture*, Vol. 1 by L. H. Bailey (New York: The MacMillan Company, 1917).

Week Six:
A Numerous Family

"A PLANT-LOUSE, we will suppose," resumed Uncle Paul, "has just established itself on the tender shoot of a rosebush. It is alone, all alone. A few days after, young plant-lice surround it: they are its sons. How many are there? Ten, twenty, a hundred? Let us say ten. Is that enough to assure the preservation of the species? Don't laugh at my question. I know well that if the plant-lice were missing from the rosebushes, the order of things would not be sensibly changed."

"The ants would be the most to be pitied," said Emile.

"The round earth would continue to turn just the same, even when the last plant-louse was dying on its leaf; but it is not, in truth, an idle question to ask if ten plant-lice suffice to preserve the race; for science has no higher object than the quest of providential means for maintaining everything in a just measure of prosperity.

"Well, ten plant-lice coming from one would be far too many if we did not have to take account of destructive agencies. One replacing one, the population remains the same; ten replacing one, in a short time the number increases beyond all possible limits. Think of the dervish's grain of wheat doubled sixty-four times, so that it becomes a bed of wheat of a finger's depth over the whole earth. What would it be if it had been multiplied ten times instead of doubled! In like manner, after a few years, the descendants of a first plant-louse, continually multiplied tenfold, would be in straitened circumstances in this world.

But there is the great reaper, death, which puts an invincible obstacle to overcrowding, counterbalances life in its overgrowing fecundity, and, in partnership with it, keeps all things in a perpetual youth. On a rosebush apparently most peaceful there is death every minute.

But the small, the humble, and weak, are the habitual pasture, the daily bread, of the large eaters. To how many dangers is not the plant-louse exposed, so tiny, so weak, and without any means of defense! No sooner does a little bird, hardly out of the shell, discover with its piercing eyes a spot haunted by the plant-lice, than, merely as an appetizer, it will swallow hundreds. And if a worm, far more rapacious, a horrible worm expressly created and put into the world to eat you alive, joins in, ah! my poor plant-lice, may God, the good God of little creatures, protect you; for your race is indeed in peril.

"Imago forms [the final stage] of ant-lion (*myrmeleon immaculate*)." Illustration by unknown artist in *Nature's Craftsmen: Popular Studies of Ants and Other Insects* by Henry C. McCook (New York and London: Harper and Brothers. 1907).

"This devourer is of a delicate green with a white stripe on its back. It is tapering in front, swollen at the back. When it doubles itself up it takes the shape of a tear-drop. They call it the ants' lion because of the ravages it makes in the stupid herd. It establishes itself among them. With its pointed mouth, it seizes one, the biggest, the plumpest; it sucks it and throws away the skin, which is too hard for it. Its pointed head is lowered again, a second plant-louse seized, raised from the leaf, and sucked. Then another and another, a twentieth, a hundredth.

The foolish herd, whose ranks are thinning, do not even seem to perceive what is going on. The trapped plant-louse kicks between the lion's fangs; the others, as if nothing were happening, continue to feed peacefully. It would take a good deal more than that to spoil their appetite! They eat while they are waiting to be eaten. The lion has had enough.

He squats amidst the herd to digest at his ease. But digestion is soon over and already the greedy worm has its eye on those that he will soon crunch. After two weeks of continual feasting, after having browsed as it were on whole herds of plant-lice, the worm turns into an elegant little dragonfly with eyes as bright as gold, and known as the *hemerobius*.

"Is that all? Oh, no. Here is the lady-bug, the good God's bug. It is round and red, with black spots. It is very pleasing; it has an innocent air. Who would take it also to be a devourer, filling its stomach with plant-lice? Look at it closely on the rosebush, and you will see it at its ferocious feasting. It is very pretty and innocent-looking; but it is a glutton, there is no denying the fact, so fond is it of plant-lice.

"Is that all? Oh, no. Those poor plant-lice are manna, the regular diet of all sorts of ravagers. Young birds eat them, the *hemerobius* eats them, lady-birds eat them, gluttons of all kinds eat them; and still there are always plant-lice. Ah! that is where, in the fight between fecundity which repairs and the rough battle of life which destroys, the weak excel by opposing legions and legions to the chances of annihilation. In vain the devourers come from all sides and pounce upon their prey; the

Lady Bird Eggs

Lady Bird

Lady Bird Pupa

Lady Bird Larva

"The Ladybird, Plate I." Illustration by unknown artist in *Beneficial Insects* by Great Britain Ministry of Agriculture and Fisheries (London : H.M. Stationary Off., 1922).

devoured survive by sacrificing a million to preserve one. The weaker they are, the more fruitful they are.

"The herring, cod, and sardine are given over as pasturage for the devourers of the sea, earth, and sky. When they undertake long voyages to graze in favorable spots, their extermination is imminent. The hungry ones of the sea surround the school of fish; the famished ones of the sky hover over their route; those of the earth await them on the shore. Man hastens to lend a strong hand to the killing and to take his share of the sea food. He equips fleets, goes to the fish with naval armies in which all nations are represented; he dries in the sun, salts, smokes, packs. But there is no perceptible diminution in the supply; for him the weak are infinite in number. One cod lays nine million eggs! Where are the devourers that will see the end of such a family?"

"Nine million eggs!" exclaimed Emile. "Is that a great many?"

"Just to count them, one by one, would take nearly a year of ten working hours each day."

"Whoever counted them had lots of patience," was Emile's comment.

"They are not counted," replied Uncle Paul; "they are weighed, which is quickly done; and from the weight the number is deduced.

"Like the cod in the sea, the plant-lice are exposed on their rosebushes and alders to numerous chances of destruction. I have told you that they are the daily bread of a multitude of eaters. So, to increase their legions, they have rapid means that are not found in other insects. Instead of laying eggs, very slow in developing, they bring forth living plant-lice, which all, absolutely all, in two weeks have obtained their growth and begin to produce another generation. This is repeated all through the season, that is to say at least half the year, so that the number of generations succeeding one another during this period cannot be less than a dozen. Let us say that one plant-louse produces ten, which is certainly below the actual number. Each of these ten plant-lice borne by the first one bears ten more, making one hundred in all; each of these hundred bears ten, in all one thousand; each of the thousand bears ten, in all ten thousand; and so on, multiplying always by ten, eleven times. Here is the same calculation as the dervish's grain of wheat, which grew with such astonishing rapidity when they multiplied it by two.

For the family of the plant-lice the increase is much more rapid, as the multiplication is made by ten. It is true that the calculation stops at the twelfth instead of going on to the sixty-fourth. No matter, the result would stupefy you; it is equal to a hundred thousand millions. To count a cod's eggs, one by one, would take nearly a year; to count the descendants of one plant-louse for six months would take ten thousand years! Where are the devourers that would see the end of the miserable louse? Guess how much space these plant-lice would cover, as closely packed as they are on the elder branch."

"Perhaps as large a place as our garden," suggested Claire.

"More than that; the garden is a hundred meters long and the same in width. Well, the family of that one plant-louse would cover a surface ten times larger; that is to say, ten hectares. What do you say to that! Is it not necessary that the young birds, little lady-bugs, and the dragonfly with the golden eyes should work hard in the extermination of the louse, which if unhindered would in a few years overrun the world?

"In spite of the hungry ones which devour them, the plant-lice seriously alarm mankind. Winged plant-lice have been seen flying in clouds thick enough to obscure the daylight. Their black legions went from one canton to another, alighted on the fruit trees, and ravaged them. Ah! when God wishes to try us, the elements are not always unchained. He sends against us in our pride the paltriest of creatures. The invisible mower, the feeble plant-louse, comes, and man is filled with fear; for the good things of the earth are in great peril.

"Man, so powerful, can do nothing against these little creatures, invincible in their multitude."

Uncle Paul finished the story of the ants and their cows. Several times since, Emile, Jules, and Claire have talked of the prodigious families of the plant-louse and the cod, but rather lost themselves in the millions and thousand millions. Their uncle was right: his stories interested them much more than Mother Ambroisine's tales.

Week Seven:
The Old Pear-Tree

UNCLE PAUL had just cut down a pear-tree in the garden. The tree was old, its trunk ravaged by worms, and for several years it had not borne any fruit. It was to be replaced by another. The children found their Uncle Paul seated on the trunk of the pear-tree. He was looking attentively at something. "One, two, three, four, five," said he, tapping with his finger upon the cross-section of the felled tree. What was he counting?

"Come quick," he called, "come; the pear-tree is waiting to tell you its story. It seems to have some curious things to tell you."

The children burst out laughing.

"And what does the old pear-tree wish to tell us!" asked Jules.

"Look here, at the cut which I was careful to make very clean with the ax. Don't you see some rings in the wood, rings which begin around the marrow and keep getting larger and larger until they reach the bark!"

"I see them," Jules replied; "they are rings fitted one inside another."

"It looks a little like the circles that come just after throwing a stone into the water," remarked Claire.

"I see them too by looking closely," chimed Emile.

"I must tell you," continued Uncle Paul, "that those circles are called annual layers. Why annual if you please? Because one is formed every year—one only, understand, neither more nor less. The learned who spend their lives studying plants, and who are called botanists, tell us that no doubt is possible on that point. From the moment the little tree springs from the seed to the time when the old tree dies, every year there is formed a ring, a layer of wood. This understood, let us count the layers of our pear-tree."

Uncle Paul took a pin to guide his counting; Emile Jules, and Claire looked on attentively. One, two three, four, five—They counted thus up to forty-five, from the marrow to the bark.

"The trunk has forty-five layers of wood," announced Uncle Paul. "Who can tell me what that signifies? How old is the pear-tree?"

"That is not very hard," answered Jules, "after what you have just told us. As it makes one ring every year, and we have counted forty-five, the pear-tree must be forty-five years old."

"Eh! Eh! what did I tell you?" cried Uncle Paul, in triumph. "Has not the pear-tree talked? It has begun its history by telling us its age. Truly, the tree is forty-five years old."

"What a singular thing!" Jules exclaimed. "You can know the age of a tree as if you saw its birth. You count the layers of wood; so many layers, so many years. One must be with you, Uncle, to learn those things. And the other trees, oak, beech, chestnut, do they do the same?"

"Absolutely the same. In our country every tree counts one year for each layer. Count its layers and you have its age."

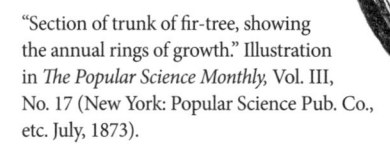

"Oh! how sorry I am I did not know that the other day," put in Emile, "when they cut down the big beech which was in the way on the edge of the road. Oh, my! What a

"Section of trunk of fir-tree, showing the annual rings of growth." Illustration in *The Popular Science Monthly*, Vol. III, No. 17 (New York: Popular Science Pub. Co., etc. July, 1873).

fine tree! It covered a whole field with its branches. It must have been very old."

"Not very," said Uncle Paul. "I counted its layers; it had one hundred and seventy."

"One hundred and seventy, Uncle Paul! Honest and truly?"

"Honest and truly, my little friend, one hundred and seventy."

"Then the beech was a hundred and seventy years old," said Jules. "Is it possible? A tree to grow so old! And no doubt it would have lived many years longer if the road-mender had not had it cut down to widen the road."

"For us, a hundred and seventy years would certainly be a great age," assented his uncle; "no one lives so long. For a tree it is very little. Let us sit down in the shade. I have more to tell you about the age of trees."

"Cedar of Lebanon." Illustration by unknown artist in *The Popular Science Monthly,* Vol. III, No. 17 (New York: Popular Science Publishing Co., 1873).

Week Seven:
The Age of Trees

"They used to tell of a chestnut of Sancerre whose trunk was more than four meters round. According to the most moderate estimate its age must have been three or four hundred years. Don't cry out at the age of this chestnut. My story is just beginning, and you may be sure that, as a narrator who stimulates the curiosity of his audience, I reserve the oldest for the end.

"Much larger chestnuts are known; for example, that of Neuve-Celle, on the borders of the Lake of Geneva, and that of Esaü, in the neighborhood of Montélimar. The first is thirteen meters round at the base of the trunk. From the year 1408 it sheltered a hermitage; the story has been testified to. Since then four centuries and a half have passed, adding to its age, and lightning has struck it at different times. No matter, it is still vigorous and full of leaves. The second is a majestic ruin. Its high branches are despoiled; its trunk, eleven meters round, is plowed with deep crevices, the wrinkles of old age. To tell the age of these two giants is hardly possible. Perhaps it might be reckoned at a thousand years, and still the two old trees bear fruit; they will not die."

"A thousand years! If Uncle had not said it, I should not believe it." This from Jules.

"Sh! You must listen to the end without saying anything," cautioned his uncle.

"The largest tree in the world is a chestnut on the slopes of Etna, in Sicily. Look at the map: you will see down there, at the extreme end of Italy, opposite the toe of that beautiful country which has the shape of a boot, a large island with three corners. That is Sicily. On that island is a celebrated mountain which throws up burning matter—a volcano, in short. It is called Etna. To come back to our chestnut, I must tell you that they call it 'the chestnut of a hundred horses,' because Jane, Queen of Aragon, visiting the volcano one day and, overtaken by a storm, took refuge under it with her escort of a hundred horsemen. Under its forest of leaves both riders and horses found shelter. To surround the giant, thirty people extending their arms and joining hands would not be enough. The trunk is more than fifty meters round. Judged by its size, it is less a tree-trunk than a fortress, a tower. An opening large enough to permit two carriages to pass abreast goes through the base of the chestnut and gives access into the cavity of the trunk, which is fitted up for the use of those who go to gather chestnuts; for the old colossus still has young sap and seldom fails to bear fruit. It is impossible to estimate the age of this giant by its size, for one suspects that a trunk as large as that comes from several chestnuts, originally distinct, but so near together that they have become welded into one.

"Great Chestnut of Mount Etna." Illustration by unknown artist in *The Popular Science Monthly*, Vol. III No. 17 (New York: Popular Science Publishing Co.1873).

"Neustadt, in Württemberg, has a linden whose branches, overburdened by years, are held up by a hundred pillars of masonry. The branches cover all together a space 130 meters in circumference. In 1229 this tree was already old, for writers of that time call it 'the big linden.' Its probable age today is seven or eight hundred years.

"There was in France, at the beginning of this century, an older tree than the veteran of Neustadt. In 1804 could be seen at the castle of Chaillé, in the Deux-Sèvres, a linden 15 meters round. It had six main branches propped with numerous pillars. If it still exists it cannot be less than eleven centuries old.

"The cemetery of Allouville, in Normandy, is shaded by one of the oldest oaks in France. The dust of the dead, into which it has thrust its roots, seems to have given it an exceptional vigor. Its trunk measures ten meters in circumference at the base. A hermit's chamber surmounted by a little steeple rises in the midst of its enormous branches.

The base of the trunk, partly hollow, is fitted up as a chapel dedicated to Our Lady of Peace. The greatest personages have esteemed it an honor to go and pray in this rustic sanctuary and meditate a moment under the shade of the old tree which has seen so many graves open and shut. According to its size, they consider this oak to be about nine hundred years old. The acorn that produced it must, then, have germinated about the year 1000. Today the old oak carries its monstrous branches without effort. Glorified by men and ravaged by lightning, it peacefully follows the course of ages, perhaps having before it a future equal to its past.

"Much older oaks are known. In 1824 a wood-cutter of Ardennes felled a gigantic oak in whose trunk were found sacrificial vases and antique coins. The old oak had had fifteen or sixteen centuries of existence.

"After the Allouville oak I will tell you of some more companions of the dead; for it is above all in these fields of repose, where the sanctity of the place protects them against the injuries of man, that the trees attain such an advanced age. Two yews in the cemetery of Haie-de-Routot, department of Eure, merit attention above all. In 1832 they shaded with their foliage the whole of the field of the dead and a part of the church, without having experienced serious damage, when an extremely violent windstorm threw a part of their branches to the ground. In spite of this mutilation these two yews are still majestic old trees. Their trunks, entirely hollow, measure each of them nine meters in circumference. Their age is estimated at fourteen hundred years.

"That, however, is not more than half the age that some other trees of the same kind have attained. A yew in a Scotch cemetery measured twenty-nine meters around. Its probable age was two thousand five hundred years. Another yew, also in a cemetery in the same country, was, in 1660, so prodigious that the whole country was talking about it. They reckoned its age then at two thousand eight hundred and twenty-four years. If it is still standing, this patriarch of European trees bears the weight of more than thirty centuries.

"Enough for the present. Now it is your turn to talk."

"I like better to be silent, Uncle Paul," said Jules. "You have upset my mind with your trees that will not die."

"I am thinking of the old yew in the Scotch cemetery. Did you say three thousand years?" asked Claire.

"Three thousand years, my dear child; and we might go still further back, if I were to tell you of certain trees in foreign countries. Some are known to be almost as old as the world."

Week Eight:
The Length of Animal Life

JULES and Claire could not get over the astonishment caused by their uncle's story of the old trees to which centuries are less than years are to us. Emile, with his usual restlessness, led the conversation to another subject:

"And animals, Uncle," asked he, "how long do they live?"

"Domestic animals," was the reply, "seldom attain the age that nature allows them. We grudge them their nourishment, overtire them, and do not give them proper shelter. And then, we take from them their milk, fleece, hide, flesh, in fact everything. How can you ever grow old when the butcher is waiting for you at the stable door with his knife? Useless to speak of these poor victims of our need: to give us long life, they do not live out their time. Supposing that an animal is well treated, that it suffers neither hunger nor cold, that it lives in peace without excessive fatigue, without fear of knacker or butcher; under these good conditions, how many years will it live?

"Let us begin with the ox. Here is a robust one, I hope. What chest and shoulders! And then that big square forehead, with its vigorous horns around which the strap of the yoke goes; those eyes shining with the serene majesty of strength. If old age is the portion of the strong, the ox ought to live for centuries."

"I should think so, too," assented Jules.

"Quite wrong, my dear children; the ox, so big, strong, massive, is old, very old, at twenty or thirty years. What to us would be verdant youth is for it decrepit old age.

"Let us pass on to the horse. You see I do not take my examples from among the weak; I choose the most vigorous. Well, the horse, as well as its modest companion, the ass, scarcely reaches more than thirty or thirty-five years."

"How mistaken I was!" Jules exclaimed. "I thought the horse and ox strong enough to live at least a century. They are so big, they take up so much room!"

"I do not know, my little friend, whether you can understand me, but I want to inform you that to take up a great deal of room in this world is not the way to live in peace and to enjoy a long life. There are people who take up a lot of space, not in the body—they are no bigger than we—but in their pretensions and their ambitious maneuvers. Do they live in peace, are they preparing for themselves a venerable old age? It is very doubtful. Let us remain small; that is to say, let us content ourselves with the little that God has given us; let us beware of the temptations of envy, the foolish counsels of pride; let us be full of activity, of work, and not of ambition. That is the only way we are permitted to hope for length of days.

"Let us return without delay to our animals. Our other domestic animals live a still shorter time. A dog, at twenty or twenty-five years, can no longer drag himself along; a pig is a tottering veteran at twenty; at fifteen at the most, a cat no longer chases mice, it says good-by to the joys of the roof and retires to some corner of a granary to die in peace; the goat and sheep, at ten or fifteen, touch extreme old age, the rabbit is at the end of its skein at eight or ten; and the miserable rat, if it lives four years, is looked upon among its own kind as a prodigy of longevity.

"Would you like me to tell you about birds?"

"Very well. The pigeon may live from six to ten years; the guinea fowl, hen, and turkey, twelve. A goose lives longer; it is true that in its quality of goose it does not worry. The goose attains twenty-five years, and even a good deal more.

"But here is something better. The goldfinch, sparrow, birds free from care, always singing, always frisking, happy as possible with a ray of sunlight in the foliage and a grain of hemp-seed, live as long as the gluttonous goose, and longer than the stupid turkey. These very happy little birds live from twenty to twenty-five years, the age of an ox. As I told you, taking up a lot of room in this world is not the way to prepare oneself for a long life.

"As to man, if he leads a regular life, he often lives to eighty or ninety. Sometimes he reaches a hundred or even more. But should he attain only the ordinary age, the average age, as they say, that is about forty, then he is to be considered a privileged creature as to length of life; the foregoing facts show it. And besides, for man, my dear children, length of life is not measured exactly according to the number of years. He lives most who works most. When God calls us to Him, let us take with us the sincere esteem of others and the consciousness of having done our duty to the end; and, whatever our age, we shall have lived long enough."

All illustrations in this chapter are by an unknown artist in *Cyclopedia of Farm Animals* by Liberty Hyde Bailey (New York: MacMillan. 1922).

Week Nine:
THE KETTLE

NOW, that day, Mother Ambroisine was very tired. She had taken down from their shelves kettles, saucepans, lamps, candlesticks, casseroles, pans, and lids. After having rubbed them with fine sand and ashes, then washed them well, she had put the utensils in the sun to dry them thoroughly. They all shone like a mirror. The kettles particularly were superb with their rosy reflections; one might have said that tongues of fire were shining inside them. The candlesticks were a dazzling yellow. Emile and Jules were lost in admiration.

"I should like to know what they make kettles of, they shine so," remarked Emile. "They are very ugly outside, all black, daubed with soot; but inside, how beautiful they are!"

"You must ask Uncle," replied his brother.

"Yes," assented Emile.

No sooner said than done: they went in search of their uncle.

"Think of the kettle with the boiling water." Illustration by unknown artist in *Home Geography for Primary Grades* by C. C. Long (New York: American Book Company, 1894).

He did not have to be entreated; he was happy whenever there was an opportunity to teach them something.

"Kettles are made of copper," he began.

"And copper?" asked Jules.

"Copper is not made. In certain countries, it is found already made, mixed with stone. It is one of the substances that it is not in the power of man to make. We use these substances as God has deposited them in the bosom of the earth for purposes of human industry; but all our knowledge and all our skill could not produce them.

"In the bosom of mountains where copper is found, they hollow out galleries which go down deep into the earth. There workmen called miners, with lamps to light them, attack the rock with great blows of the pick, while others carry the detached blocks outside. These blocks of stone in which copper is found are called ore. In furnaces made for the purpose, they heat the ore to a very high temperature. The heat of our stove, when it is red-hot, is nothing in comparison. The copper melts, runs, and is separated from the rest. Then, with hammers of enormous weight, set in motion by a wheel turned by water, they strike the mass of copper which, little by little, becomes thin and is hollowed into a large basin.

"The coppersmith continues the work. He takes the shapeless basin and, with little strokes of the hammer, fashions it on the anvil to give it a regular shape."

"That is why coppersmiths tap all day with their hammers," commented Jules. "I had often wondered, when passing their shops, why they made so much noise, always tapping, without any stop. They were thinning the copper; shaping it into saucepans and kettles."

Here Emile asked: "When a kettle is old, has holes in it and can't be used, what do they do with it? I heard Mother Ambroisine speak of selling a worn out kettle."

"It is melted, and another new kettle made out of the copper," replied Uncle Paul.

"Then the copper does not wear away!"

"It wears away too much, my friend: some of it is lost when they rub it with sand to make it shine; some is lost, too, by the continual action of the fire; but what is left is still good."

"Mother Ambroisine also spoke of recasting a lamp which had lost a foot. What are lamps made of?"

"They are of tin, another substance that we find ready-made in the bosom of the earth, without the power of producing it ourselves.

(OPPOSITE) "A mine is like a great cavern." Illustration by unknown artist in *Home Geography for Primary Grades* by C. C. Long (New York: American Book Company, 1894).

(FROM LEFT, CLOCKWISE): Copper kettle, brass candlesticks, silver ewer, and gold coin. All images courtesy of the Metropolitan Museum of Art.

Week Nine:
Metals

"COPPER and tin are called metals," continued Uncle Paul. "They are heavy, shining substances, which bear the blows of the hammer without breaking. They flatten, but do not break. There are still other substances which possess the considerable weight of copper and tin, as well as their brilliancy and resistance to blows. All these substances are called metals."

"Then lead, which is so heavy, is a metal too?" asked Emile.

"Iron also, silver and gold?" queried his brother.

"Yes, these substances and still others are metals. All have a peculiar brilliancy called metallic luster, but the color varies. Copper is red; gold, yellow; silver, iron, lead, tin, white, with a very slightly different shade one from another."

"The candlesticks Mother Ambroisine is drying in the sun," said Emile, "are a magnificent yellow and so shiny they dazzle. Are they gold?"

"No, my dear child; your uncle does not possess such riches. They are brass. To vary the colors and other properties of the metals, instead of always using them separately, they often mix two or three together, or even more. They melt them together, and the whole constitutes a sort of new metal, different from those which enter into its composition. Thus, in melting together copper and a kind of white metal called zinc, the same as the garden watering pots are made of, they obtain brass, which has not the red of copper, nor the white of zinc, but the yellow of gold. The material of the candlesticks is, then, made of copper and zinc together; in a word, it is brass, and not gold, in spite of its luster and yellow color. Gold is yellow and glitters; but all that is yellow and glitters is not gold. At the last village fair they sold magnificent rings whose brilliancy deceived you. In gold, they would have cost a fine sum. The merchant sold them for a sou. They were brass."

"How can they tell gold from brass, since the color and luster are almost the same!" asked Jules.

"By the weight, chiefly. Gold is much heavier than brass; it is indeed the heaviest metal in frequent use. After it comes lead, then silver, copper, iron, tin, and finally zinc, the lightest of all."

"You told us that to melt copper," put in Emile, "they needed a fire so intense, that the heat of a red-hot stove would be nothing in comparison. All metals do not resist like that, for I remember very well in what a sorry way the first leaden soldiers you gave me came to their end. Last winter, I had lined them up on the luke-warm stove. Just when I was not watching, the troop tottered, sank down, and ran in little streams of melted lead. I had only time to save half a dozen grenadiers, and their feet were missing."

"And when Mother Ambroisine thoughtlessly put the lamp on the stove," added Jules, "oh! it was soon done for: a finger's breadth of tin had disappeared."

"Tin and lead melt very easily," explained Uncle Paul. "The heat of our hearth is enough to make them run. Zinc also melts without much trouble; but silver, then copper, then gold, and finally iron, need fires of an intensity unknown in our houses. Iron, above all, has excessive resistance, very valuable to us.

"Shovels, tongs, grates, stoves, are iron. These various objects, always in contact with the fire, do not melt, however; do not even soften. To soften iron, so as to shape it easily on the anvil by blows from the hammer, the smith needs all the heat of his forge. In vain would he blow and put on coal; he would never succeed in melting it.

Iron, however, can be melted, but you must use the most intense heat that human skill can produce. "

76 *Exploring Insects with Uncle Paul*

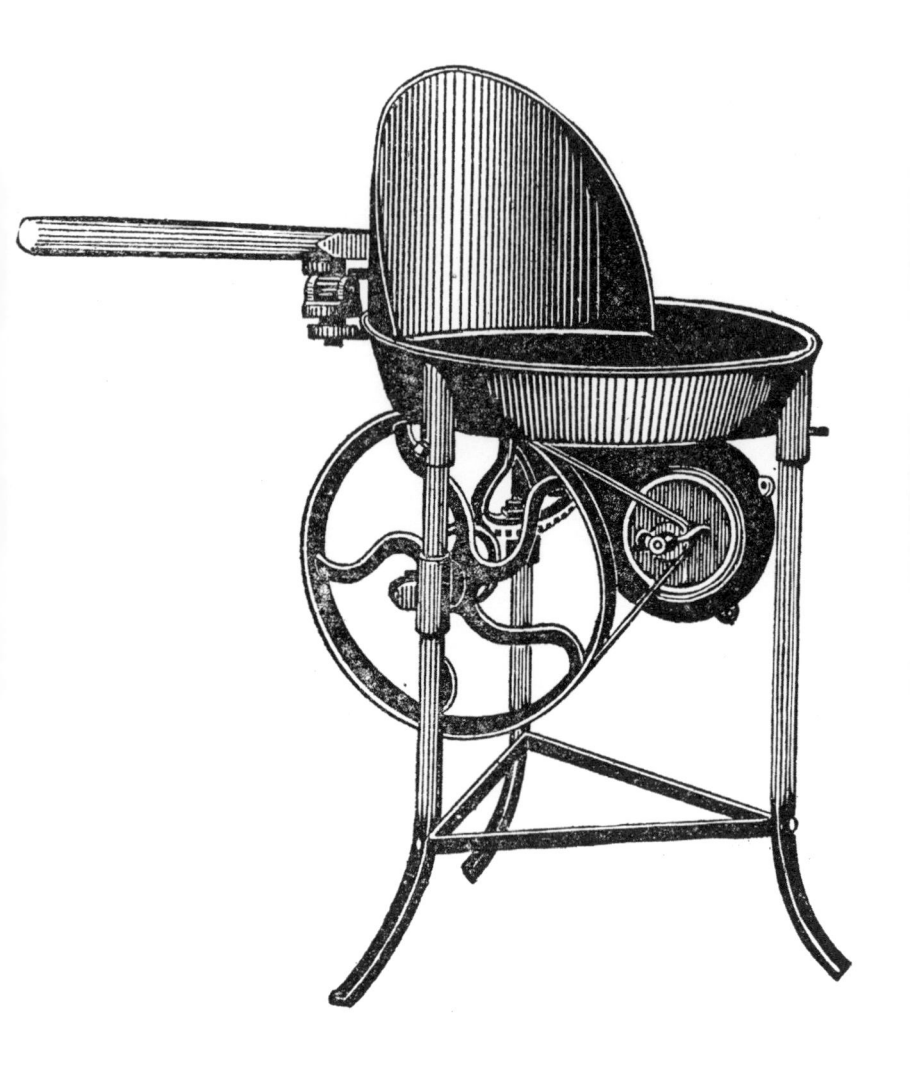

"A wagon comprised to carry the essential equipment for blacksmiths and artisans to perform their work." Illustration by unknown artist in *Farm Economy* by The Federal Digest (Minneapolis, MN: Better Farming Association, 1921).

Week Ten:
Metal Plating

In the morning some wandering coppersmiths were passing. Mother Ambroisine had sold them the old kettle. Besides the sale, they were to make over the lamp whose foot had melted on the stove, and replate two saucepans. So the smiths lighted a fire in the open air, set up their bellows on the ground, and in a large round iron spoon melted the old lamp, adding a little tin to replace what had been lost. The melted metal was run into a mold, from which it came out in the shape of a lamp. This lamp, still pretty large, was fixed on a lathe which a little boy set in motion; and while it turned, the master touched it with the edge of a steel tool. The tin thus planed off fell in thin shavings, rolled up like curl-papers. The lamp was visibly becoming perfect; it took the proper polish and shape.

Afterward they busied themselves plating the copper saucepans. They cleaned them thoroughly inside with sand, put them on the fire, and, when they were very hot, went over the whole of their surface with a tow pad and a little melted tin. Wherever the pad rubbed, the tin stuck to the copper. In a few moments the inside of the saucepan, red before, was now shiny white.

Emile and Jules, while eating their little lunch of apples and bread, looked on at this curious work without saying a word. They promised themselves to ask their uncle the reason for whitening the inside of the copper saucepans with tin. In the evening, accordingly, they spoke of the tinning and plating.

"Highly cleaned and polished iron is very brilliant," explained their uncle. "The blade of a new knife, Claire's scissors, carefully kept in their case, are examples. But, if exposed to damp air, iron tarnishes quickly and covers itself with an earthy and red crust called—"

"Rust," interposed Claire.

"Yes, it is called rust."

"The big nails that hold the iron wires where the bell-flowers climb up the garden wall are covered with that red crust," remarked Jules; and Emile added:

"The old knife I found in the ground is covered with it too."

"Those large nails and the old knife are encrusted with rust because they have remained for a long time exposed to the air and dampness. Damp air corrodes iron; it becomes incorporated with the metal and makes it unrecognizable. When rusty, iron no longer has the properties that make it so useful to us; it is a kind of red or yellow earth, in which, without looking attentively, it would be impossible to suspect a metal."

"I can well believe it," said Jules. "For my part, I should never have taken rust for iron with which air and moisture had become incorporated."

"Many other metals rust like iron; that is to say, they are converted into earthy matter by contact with damp air. The color of rust varies according to the metal. Iron rust is yellow or red, that of copper is green, lead and zinc white."

"Then the green rust of old pennies is copper rust," said Jules.

"The white matter that covers the nozzle of the pump must be lead rust!" queried Claire.

"Exactly. The prime difficulty with rust is that it makes metals ugly: they lose their brilliance and polish; but it works still greater injury. There are harmless rusts which might get mixed with our food without danger: such is iron rust. On the contrary, copper and lead rusts are deadly poisons. If, by mischance, these rusts should get into our food, we might die, or at least we should experience cruel suffering.

We will speak only of copper, for lead, on account of its quick melting, cannot go on the fire and is not used for kitchen utensils. Copper rust, I say, is a mortal poison; and yet they prepare food in copper vessels. Ask Mother Ambroisine."

"Very true," said she, "but I always have my eye on my saucepans: I keep them very clean and from time to time have them re-plated."

"I don't understand," put in Jules, "how the work that the tinsmith did this morning could prevent the copper rust being a poison."

"The smith's work will not make the copper rust cease to be a poison," replied Uncle Paul, "but it will prevent the rust's forming. Of the common metals tin rusts the least. Exposed to the air a long time, it scarcely tarnishes. And then the rust, which forms in small quantities, is innocuous, like iron rust. To prevent copper from covering itself with poisonous green spots, to preserve it from rust, it must be kept from contact with damp air and also with certain alimentary substances such as vinegar, oil, grease—substances that provoke the rapid formation of rust. For this reason the copper saucepan is coated over with tin inside. Under the thin bed of tin which covers it, the copper cannot rust, because it is no longer in contact with the air. The tin remains; but this metal changes with difficulty, and, besides, its rust, if it forms any, is harmless. So they plate copper, that is to say they cover it with a thin bed of tin, to prevent its rusting, and thus to prevent the formation of the dangerous poison that might, some day or other, be mixed with our food.

"They also tin iron, not to prevent the formation of poison, for the rust of this metal is harmless, but simply to preserve it from changing and covering itself with ugly red spots. This tinned iron is called tinplate. Lids, coffee-pots, dripping-pans, graters, lanterns, and innumerable other things, are of tinplate; that is to say, thin sheets of iron covered on both sides with a coating of tin."

"They take the gravel and dirt to the sides of the streams, and roll it about in wooden bowls. After a while there is nothing but the gold and the gravel. The miners throw the gravel away handful by handful." Illustration by unknown artist in *Carpenter's Geographical Reader: South America* by Frank G. Carpenter (New York, American Book Company, 1915).

Week Ten:
Gold and Iron

"Some metals never rust; such a one is gold. Ancient gold pieces found in the earth after centuries are as bright as the day they were coined. No dross, no rust covers their effigy and inscription. Time, fire, humidity, air, cannot harm this admirable metal. Therefore gold, on account of its unchangeable luster and its rarity, is preeminently the material for ornaments and coins.

"Furthermore, gold is the first metal that man became acquainted with, long before iron, lead, tin, and the others. The reason why man's attention was called to gold, long centuries before iron, is not hard to understand. Gold never rusts; iron rusts with such grievous facility that in a short time, if we are not careful, it is converted into a red earth.

I have just told you that gold objects, however old they may be, have come to us intact, even after having been in the dampest ground. As for objects of iron, not one has reached us that was not in an unrecognizable state. Corroded with rust, they have become a shapeless earthy crust. Now I will ask Jules if the iron ore that is extracted from the bowels of the earth can be real, pure iron, such as we use."

"It seems to me not, Uncle; for if iron at any given moment is pure, it must rust with time and change to earthy matter, as does the blade of a knife buried in the ground."

"My brother seems to reason correctly; I agree with him," said Claire.

"And gold?" Uncle Paul asked her.

"It is different with gold," she replied. "As that metal never rusts, is not changed by time, air, and dampness, it must be pure."

"Exactly so. In the rocks where it is disseminated in small scales, gold is as brilliant as in jewelers' boxes. Claire's earrings have not more luster than the particles set by nature in the rock. On the contrary, what a pitiful appearance iron makes when it is found! It is an earthy crust, a reddish stone, in which only after long research can one suspect the presence of a metal; it is, in fact, rust, mixed more or less with other substances. And then, it is not enough to perceive that this rusty stone contains a metal; a way must still be found to decompose the ore and bring the iron back to its metallic state. How many efforts were necessary to attain this result, one of the most difficult to achieve! How many fruitless attempts, how many painful trials! Iron, then, was the last to become of use to us, long after gold and other metals, like copper and silver, which are sometimes, but not always, found pure. That most useful of metals was the last; but with it an immense advance was made in human industry. From the moment man was in possession of iron, he found himself master of the earth.

"At the head of substances that resist shock, iron must be placed; and it is precisely its enormous resistance to rupture that makes this metal so precious to us. Never would a gold, copper, marble, or stone anvil resist the blows of the smith's hammer as an iron one does. The hammer itself, of what substance other than iron could it be made? If of copper, silver, or gold, it would flatten, crush, and become useless in a short time; for these metals lack hardness. If of stone, it would break at the first rather hard blow. For these implements nothing can take the place of iron. Nor can it for axes, saws, knives, the mason's chisel, the quarry-man's pick, the plowshare, and a number of other implements which cut, hew, pierce, plane, file, give or receive violent blows. Iron alone has the hardness that can cut most other substances, and the resistance that sets blows at defiance. In this respect iron is, of all mineral substances, the handsomest present that Providence has given to man. It is preeminently the material for tools, indispensable in every art and industry."

"Claire and I read one day," said Jules, "that when the Spaniards discovered America, the men of that new country had gold axes, which they very willingly exchanged for iron ones. I laughed at their innocence, which made them give such a costly price for a piece of very common metal. I think I see now that the exchange was to their advantage."

"Yes, decidedly to their advantage; for with an iron ax they could fell trees to make their dug-out canoes and their huts; they could better defend themselves against wild animals and attack the game in their hunts. This piece of iron gave them an assurance of food, a substantial boat, a warm dwelling, a redoubtable weapon. In comparison, a gold ax was only a useless plaything."

"If iron came last, what did men do before they knew of it?" asked Jules.

"They made their weapons and tools of copper; for, like gold, this metal is sometimes in a pure state so that it can be utilized just as nature gives it to us. But a copper implement, having little hardness, is of much less value than an iron one. Thus, in those far-off days of copper axes, man was indeed a wretched creature.

"He was still more so before knowing copper. He cut a flint into a point, or split it, and fastened it to the end of a stick; and that was his only weapon.

"With this stone he had to procure food, clothing, a hut, and to defend himself from wild beasts. His clothing was a skin thrown over his back, his dwelling a hut made of twisted branches

"An Iron Mine." Illustration by unknown artist in *Home Geography for Primary Grades* by C. C. Long (New York: American Book Company, 1894).

and mud; his food a piece of flesh, produce of the chase. Domestic animals were unknown, the earth uncultivated, all industry lacking."

"And where was that?" asked Claire.

"Everywhere, my dear child; here, even in places where today are our most flourishing towns. Oh! how forlorn man was before attaining, by the help of iron, the well-being that we enjoy today; how forlorn was man and what a great present Providence made him in giving him this metal!"

Just as Uncle Paul finished, Jacques knocked discreetly at the door; Jules ran to open it. They whispered a few words to each other. It was about an important affair for the next day.

"From what animal do we get wool?" Illustration by unknown artist in *Home Geography for Primary Grades* by C. C. Long (New York: American Book Company, 1894).

Week Eleven:
THE FLEECE

AS was agreed upon the day before, Jacques made ready for the performance. To keep the patients from moving, they were obliged to make them lie down, their feet tied, between the two inclined planks of a rack. Steel knives shone on the ground. As for them, innocent victims of the needs of man, they were already bound and lying on their sides. With gentle resignation they awaited their sad fate. Were they going to be slain? Oh, no: they were to be shorn. Jacques took a sheep by its feet, placed it between the two planks of the rack, and, with large scissors, began, cra-cra-cra, to cut off the wool. Little by little, the fleece fell all in one piece. When the sheep had been despoiled, it ran free to one side, ashamed and chilly. It had just given its covering to clothe man. Jacques put another one on the rack, and the scissors began to move.

"Tell me, Jacques," said Jules, "are not the sheep very cold when they have had their wool cut off? See how that one trembles that you have just shorn."

"Never mind that: I have chosen a fine day for it. The sun is warm. By tomorrow they won't feel the need of their wool. And besides, ought not the sheep to suffer a little cold so that we may be warm?"

"We warm? How?"

"You astonish me. You do not know that, you who read so many books! Well, with this wool they will make you stockings and knitted things for this winter; they will even make cloth, fine cloth for clothes."

"Peuh!" exclaimed Emile. "This wool is too dirty and ugly to make stockings, knitted things, and cloth."

"Dirty at present," Jacques agreed, "but it will be washed in the river, and when it has become very white Mother Ambroisine will work it on her spinning-wheel and make yarn of it. This yarn, knitted with needles, will become stockings that one is very glad to have on one's feet when obliged to run in the snow."

"I have never seen red, green, blue sheep; and yet there are red, green, blue, and other colored wools," said Emile.

"They dye the white wool that the sheep gives us; they put it into boiling water with drugs and coloring matter, and it comes out of that water with a color that stays."

"And cloth!"

"And cloth is made with threads of wool like those of stockings; but in order to weave these threads, make them cross each other regularly, and convert them into fabric, you must have complicated machines, weaving looms that cannot be had in our houses. These are only found in large factories used for manufacturing woolen goods."

"Then these trousers that I have on come from the sheep;

this vest; my cravat, stockings too. I am dressed in the spoils of the sheep!" This from Jules.

"Yes, to defend ourselves from the cold, we take the sheep's wool. The poor beast furnishes its fleece for our clothes, its milk and flesh for our nourishment, its skin for our gloves. We live on the life of our domestic animals. The ox gives us his strength, flesh, hide; the cow, besides, gives us milk. The donkey, mule, horse, work for us. As soon as they are dead they leave us their skin, of which we make leather for our shoes. The hen gives us eggs, the dog puts his intelligence at our service. And yet there are people who, without any motive, maltreat these animals without which we should be so poor, who let them suffer hunger and beat them unmercifully! Never imitate those heartless ones; it would be an insult to God, who has given us the donkey, ox, sheep, and other animals. When I think that these valuable creatures give us all, even to their very life, I would share my last crust with them."

And the shears meanwhile continued their cra-cra-cra, and the fleece fell.

(OPPOSITE PAGE, TOP) "Hand cards" and "Spinning Wheel." Illustrations by unknown artist in *The Story of Textiles* by Newark Museum Association (Self-published, 1916).

(OPPOSITE PAGE, BOTTOM) "Hargreave's Spinning Jenny." Illustration by unknown artist in *Textiles and Clothing* by Ellen A. McGowan and Charlotte A. Waite (New York: Macmillan. 1919).

(ABOVE) "An Improved Southdown Sheep Type." Illustration by unknown artist in *Cyclopedia of Farm Animals* by Liberty Hyde Bailey (New York: MacMillan, 1922).

88   *Exploring Insects with Uncle Paul*

"Leaf and flowers of the hemp plant (Cannabis sativa). A and c are female flowers, while b is a male flower." Illustration by unknown artist in *Southern Field Crops* by J.F. Duggar, (New York: MacMillan Company, 1911).

Week Eleven:
Flax and Hemp

WHILE listening to what Jacques was saying about wool, Emile examined his handkerchief attentively. He turned it over and over, felt it, then looked through it. Jacques foresaw the question Emile was getting ready to ask him, and he said:

"Handkerchiefs and linens are not woolen. Certain plants, cotton, hemp, flax, and not sheep, furnish them; for, you see, I don't know much about those things myself. I have heard tell of the cotton plant, but have never seen it. And, besides, I am afraid talking to you will make me cut the sheep's skin."

In the evening, at Jules's request, they took up the history of the materials with which we clothe ourselves, and Uncle Paul explained their nature.

"The outside of hemp and flax is composed of long threads, very fine, supple, and tenacious, from which we manufacture our fabrics. We clothe ourselves with the spoils of the sheep; we make ourselves fine with the bark of the plant. The fabrics of luxury, cambric, tulle, gauze, point-lace, Mechlin lace, are made from flax; the stronger ones, even to coarse sacking, are of hemp. The cotton plant gives us the fabrics made of cotton.

"Flax is a slender plant with little delicate blue flowers, and is sown and harvested every year. It is much cultivated in Northern France, Belgium, and Holland. It is the first plant used by man for woven fabrics.

Mummies of Egypt, the old land of Moses and the patriarchs, mummies which have lain buried four thousand years and more, are swathed in bands of linen."

"Mummies, did you say?" interposed Jules. "I don't know what they are."

"I will tell you, my dear child. Respect for the dead is found among all people and in all ages. Man regards as sacred what was the seat of a soul made in the image of God; he honors the dead, but the honors rendered differ according to time, place, customs. We inter the dead and put over the burial place a tombstone with an inscription, or at least a humble cross, divine emblem of life eternal. The ancients burned them on a funeral pyre; they piously gathered the bones bleached by the fire and enclosed them in priceless vases. In Egypt, to preserve the cherished remains for the family, they embalmed the dead; that is to say, they impregnated them with aromatics and swathed them in linen to prevent decomposition. These pious duties were so delicately performed that, after centuries and centuries, we find intact in their chests of sweet-smelling wood, but dried and blackened by years, contemporaries of the ancient kings of Egypt, or the Pharaohs. These are what are called mummies.

"Hemp has been cultivated all over Europe for many centuries. It is an annual, of a strong, nauseous odor, with little, green, dull-looking flowers, whose stem, of the thickness of a quill pen, rises to about two meters. It is cultivated, like flax, both for its bark and for its grain, called hemp-seed."

"That is the grain, I think," said Emile, "we give the goldfinch, which it cracks with its beak when it breaks the shell to get out the little kernel."

"Yes, hemp-seed is the feast of little birds.

"The bark of the hemp has not the fineness of flax. The fibers of this latter plant are so fine that twenty-five grams of tow spun on the

"Flax is a small plant." Illustration by unknown artist in *Home Geography for Primary Grades* by C. C. Long (New York: American Book Company, c. 1894).

spinning wheel furnishes a thread almost a league long. The spider's web alone can rival in delicacy certain linen fabrics.

"When hemp and flax reach maturity, they are harvested, and the seeds are separated by threshing. The next operation, retting, then takes place, its purpose being to render the filaments of the bark, or the fibers, as they are called, easily separable from the wood. These fibers, in fact, are pasted to the stem and stuck together by a gummy substance that is very resistant and prevents separation until it is destroyed by rot. They sometimes do this retting by spreading the plants in the fields for a couple of weeks and turning them over now and then, until the tow detaches itself from the woody part or hemp stalk.

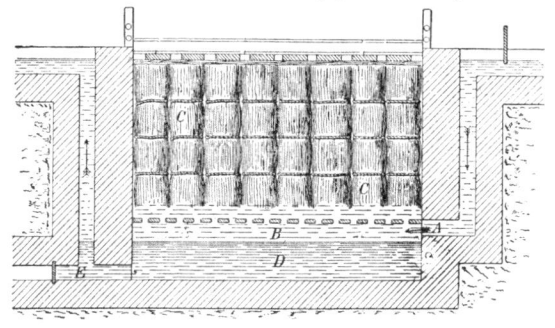

"RETTING TANK: *A*–Inlet; *B*—Undisturbed Water; *C*—Bundles of Flax." Illustration by unknown artist in T*extiles and Clothing* by Kate Heintz Watson (Chicago: American School of Home Economics. 1914).

"But the quickest way is to tie the flax and hemp in bundles and keep them submerged in a pond. There soon follows a rot which gives out intolerable smells; the bark decays, and the fiber, endowed with exceptional resistance, is freed.

"Then the bundles are dried; after that they crush them between the jaws of an instrument called a brake, to crush the stems into small pieces and separate the tow. Finally, to purge the tow of all woody refuse and to divide it into the finest threads, they pass it between the iron teeth of a sort of big comb called a heckle. In this state, the fiber is spun either by hand or by machine. The thread obtained is ready for weaving.

"On a loom they place in order, side by side, numerous threads composing what they call the warp.

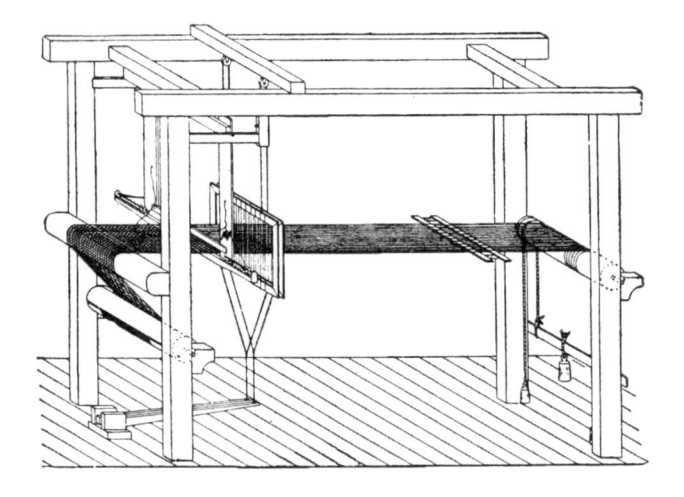

By turns, impelled by a pedal on which the operator's foot presses, one half of these threads descends while the other half ascends. At the same time the operator passes a transverse thread in a shuttle through the two halves of the warp, from left to right, then from right to left. From this inter-crossing comes the woven fabric. And it is finished; the garb of the plant has changed masters; the bark of the hemp has become cloth, that of flax a princely lace worth some hundreds of francs by the piece."

"Colonial Hand Loom." Illustration by unknown artist in *The Story of Textiles* by Newark Museum Association (Newark: Self-Published, 1916).

Week Twelve:
Cotton

COTTON, the most important of the materials used for our woven fabrics, is furnished by a semi-tropical plant called the cotton plant. It is an herb or even a shrub from one to two meters high, and its large yellow flowers are followed by an abundant fruitage of bolls, each as large as an egg, filled with a silky flock, sometimes brilliantly white, sometimes a pale yellowish shade, according to the kind of cotton. In the middle of this flock are the seeds."

"Cotton flowers" Illustration by unknown artist in *Flore Forestiere: Arbres et Arbustes due Centre de L'Europe.* Edited by J. Rothschild (London: The Botanical Society of France and Geological Society of London Booksellers: 1872).

"It seems to me I have seen flock of that kind fall in flakes in the spring from the top of poplars and willows," said Claire.

"The comparison is very good. Willows and poplars have for their fruit tiny little long and pointed bolls three or four times as large as a pin's head. In the month of May these bolls are ripe. They open and set free a very fine white down, in the middle of which are the seeds. If the air is calm, this down piles up at the foot of the tree in a bed of cotton wool, as white as snow; but at the least breath of wind the flakes are borne long distances, carrying with them the seeds, which thus find unoccupied places where they can germinate and become trees. Many other seeds are provided with soft aigrettes, silky plumes, which keep them up in the air a long time and permit them distant journeys in order to disseminate the plant. For example, who is not familiar with the seeds of thistles and dandelions, those beautiful silky plumed seeds that you take pleasure in blowing into the air?"

"Can the flock of poplar bolls be put to the same use as cotton?" Jules asked.

"By no means. There is too little of it, and it would be too difficult to gather. Besides, it is so short it might not be possible to spin it. But if we ourselves cannot make use of it, others find it very useful. This flock is the little birds' cotton; many gather it to line their nests. The goldfinch, among others, is one of the cleverest of the clever. Its house of cotton is a masterpiece of elegance and solidity. In the fork of several little branches, with the cottony flock of the willow and poplar, with bits of wool that hedge thorns pull out from sheep as they pass, with the plumy aigrettes of thistle seeds, it makes for its young a cup-shaped mattress, so soft and warm and wadded that no little prince in his swaddling-clothes ever had the like.

"To build their nests, birds find materials near at hand; they only have to set to work. When spring comes, the goldfinch does not have to think of the materials for its nest; it is sure that the osierbeds, thistles, and roadside hedges will furnish in abundance all that it needs. And it ought to be thus, for a bird has not the intelligence to prepare a long time in advance, by careful and wise industry, the things that it will need. Man, whose noble prerogative it is to acquire everything by work and reflection, procures cotton from distant countries; a bird finds its cotton on the poplars of its grove.

"At maturity the cotton bolls open wide, and their flock bursts out in soft flakes that are gathered by hand, boll by boll. The flock, well dried in the sun on screens, is beaten with flails or, better, submitted to the action of certain machines. It is thus freed from all seeds and husks. Without any other preparation, cotton comes to us in large bales to be converted into fabrics in our manufactories. The countries that furnish the most of it are India, Egypt, Brazil, and, above all, the United States of North America.

"In a single year the European manufactories work up nearly eight hundred million kilograms of cotton. This enormous weight is not too much, for the whole world clothes itself with the precious flock, turned into print, percale, calico. Thus human activity has no greater field than the cotton trade. How many workmen, how many delicate operations, what long voyages, all for a simple piece of print costing a few centimes! A handful of cotton is gathered, we will suppose, two or three thousand leagues from here. This cotton crosses the ocean, goes a quarter round the globe, and comes to France or England to be manufactured. Then it is spun, woven, ornamented with colored designs, and, converted into print, crosses the seas again, to go perhaps to the other end of the world to serve as head-dress. What a multiplicity of interests are brought into play! It was necessary to sow the plant; then, for a good half of the year, to cultivate it. Out of a handful of flock, then, provision must be made for the remuneration of those who have cultivated and harvested. Next come the dealer who buys and the mariner who transports it. To each of them is due a part of the handful of flock. Then follow the spinner, weaver, dyer, all of whom the cotton must indemnify for their work. It is far from being finished. Now come other dealers who buy the fabrics, other mariners who carry them to all parts of the world, and finally merchants who sell them at retail. How can the handful of flock pay all these interested ones without itself acquiring an exorbitant price?

"To accomplish this wonder two industrial powers intervene: work on a large scale and the aid of machinery. You have seen how Ambroisine spins wool on the wheel. The carded wool is first divided into long locks. One of these locks is applied to a hook which turns rapidly. The hook seizes the wool and in its rotation twists the fibers

"Cotton Bales." Illustration by unknown artist in *Textiles and Clothing* by Kate Heintz Watson (Chicago: American School of Home Economics, 1914).

into one thread, which lengthens little by little at the expense of the lock held and regulated by the fingers. When the thread attains a certain length, Mother Ambroisine rolls it on the spindle by a suitable movement of the wheel; then she continues twisting the wool again.

"Strictly speaking, cotton could be spun in the same way; but, however clever Mother Ambroisine may be, the fabrics made from the thread of her wheel would cost an enormous price on account of the time spent. What, then, is to be done! A machine is made to spin the cotton. In rooms larger than the biggest church are placed, by hundreds of thousands, the nicely adjusted machines proper for spinning, with hooks, spindles, and bobbins. And all turn at the same time with a precision and rapidity that defy watching. The work goes on with noise enough to deafen you. The flock of cotton is seized by thousands and thousands of hooks; the endless threads come and go from one bobbin to another, and roll themselves on the spindles. In a few hours a mountain of cotton is converted into thread, the length of which would go several times around the whole earth. What have they spent for work which would have exhausted the strength of an army of spinners as clever as Mother Ambroisine? Some shovelfuls of coal to heat the water, the steam of which starts the machine that sets everything going. Weaving, the printing of the colored designs,—in short, the various operations that the flock undergoes to become cloth are executed by means quite as expeditious, quite as economical. And it is thus that the planter, broker, mariner, spinner, weaver, dyer, and merchant can all have their share in the handful of cotton flock which has become a piece of calico and is sold for four sous."

"Swallowtail Butterflies" (as well as other images in this chapter). Illustrations by unknown artist in *The Butterfly Book* by William J. Holland (New York: Doubleday & McClure Co., 1898).

Week Thirteen:
Butterflies

OH, how beautiful! Oh, my goodness, how beautiful they are! There are some whose wings are barred with red on a garnet background; some bright blue with black circles; others are sulphur yellow with orange spots; again others are white fringed with gold-color. They have on the forehead two fine horns, two antennae, sometimes fringed like an aigrette, sometimes cut off like a tuft of feathers. Under the head they have a proboscis, a sucker as fine as a hair and twisted into a spiral. When they approach a flower, they untwist the proboscis and plunge it to the bottom of the corolla to drink a drop of honeyed liquor. Oh, how beautiful they are! Oh, my goodness, how beautiful they are! But if one manages to touch them, their wings tarnish and leave between the fingers a fine dust like that of precious metals.

Now their uncle told the children the names of the butterflies that flew on the flowers in the garden. "This one," said he, whose wings are white with a black border and three black spots, is called the cabbage butterfly. This larger one, whose yellow wings barred with black terminate in a long tail, at the base of which are found a large rust-colored eye and blue spots, is called the swallow-tail. This tiny one, sky-blue above, silver-gray underneath, sprinkled with black eyes in white circles, with a line of reddish spots bordering the wings, is called the Argus."

And Uncle Paul continued thus, naming the butterflies that a bright sun had drawn to the flowers.

"The Argus ought to be difficult to catch," observed Emile. "He sees everywhere; his wings are covered with eyes."

"The pretty round spots that a great many butterflies have on their wings are not really eyes, although they are called by that name; they are ornaments, nothing more. Real eyes, eyes for seeing, are in the head. The Argus has two, neither more nor fewer than the other butterflies."

"Claire tells me," said Jules, "that butterflies come from caterpillars. Is it true, Uncle?"

"Yes, my child. Every butterfly, before becoming the graceful creature which flies from flower to flower with magnificent wings, is an ugly caterpillar that creeps with effort. Thus the cabbage butterfly, which I have just shown you, is first a green caterpillar, which stays on the cabbages and gnaws the leaves. Jacques will tell you how much pains he takes to protect his cabbage patch from the voracious insect; for, you see, caterpillars have a terrible appetite. You will soon learn the reason.

Caterpillar of *Callidryas eubule*

"Most insects behave like caterpillars. On coming out of the egg, they have a provisional form that they must replace later by another. They are, as it were, born twice: first imperfect, dull, voracious, ugly; then perfect, agile, abstemious, and often of an admirable richness and elegance. Under its first form, the insect is a worm called by the general name of larva.

"You remember the lion of the plant-lice, the grub that eats the lice of the rosebush and, for weeks, without being able to satisfy itself, continues night and day its ferocious feasting. Well, this grub is a larva, that will change itself into a little lace-winged fly, the *hemerobius*, whose wings are of gauze and eyes of gold. Before becoming the pretty red ladybird with black spots, this pretty insect, which, in spite of its innocent air, crunches the plant-lice, is a very ugly worm—a slate-colored larva, covered with little points, and itself very fond of plant-lice. The June bug, the silly June bug, which, if its leg is held by a thread, awkwardly puffs out its wings, makes all preparations, and starts out to the tune of 'Fly, fly, fly!' is at first a white worm, a plump larva, fat as bacon, which lives underground, attacks the roots of plants, and destroys our crops. The big stag-beetle, whose head is armed with menacing mandibles shaped like the stag's horns, is at first a large worm that lives in old tree-trunks. It is the same with the Capricorn, so peculiar for its long antennae. And the worm found in our ripe cherries, which is so repugnant to us, what does it become? It becomes a beautiful fly, its wings adorned with four bands of black velvet. And so on with others.

"Well, this initial state of the insect, this worm, first form of youth, is called the larva. The wonderful change which transforms the larva into a perfect insect is called metamorphosis. Caterpillars are larvae. By metamorphosis they turn into those beautiful butterflies whose wings, decorated with the richest colors, fill us with admiration. The Argus, now so beautiful with its celestial blue wings, was first a poor hairy caterpillar; the splendid swallowtail began by being a green caterpillar with black stripes across it and red spots on its sides. Out of these despicable vermin metamorphosis has made those delightful creatures which only the flowers can rival in elegance.

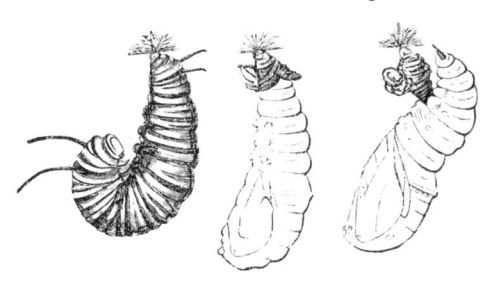

Caterpillar of *Anosia plexippus*, undergoing change into chrysalis

"You all know the tale of Cinderella. The sisters have left for the ball, very proud, very smart. Cinderella, her heart full, is watching the kettle. The godmother arrives. 'Go,' says she, 'to the garden and get a pumpkin.' And behold, the scooped-out pumpkin changes under the godmother's wand, into a gilded carriage. 'Cinderella,' says she again, 'open the mouse-trap.' Six mice run out of it, and are no sooner touched by the magic wand than they turn into six beautiful dappled-gray horses. A bearded rat becomes a big coachman with a commanding mustache. Six lizards sleeping behind the watering pot become green bedizened [gaudily dressed] footmen, who immediately jump up behind the carriage. Finally the poor girl's shabby clothes are changed to gold and silver ones sprinkled with precious stones. Cinderella starts for the ball, in glass slippers. You, apparently, know the rest of it better than I.

"These powerful godmothers for whom it is play to change mice into horses, lizards into footmen, ugly clothes into sumptuous ones, these gracious fairies who astonish you with their fabulous prodigies, what are they, my dear children, in comparison with reality, the great fairy of the good God, who, out of a dirty worm, object of disgust, knows how to make a creature of ravishing beauty? He touches with his divine wand a miserable hairy caterpillar, an abject worm that slobbers in rotten wood, and the miracle is accomplished: the disgusting larva has turned into a beetle all shining with gold, a butterfly whose azure wings would have outshone Cinderella's fine toilette."

Week Fourteen:
The Big Eaters

"INSECTS propagate themselves by eggs, which they lay, with admirable foresight, where the young will be sure to find nourishment. The little creature that comes from the egg is a larva, a feeble grub, which, most often, has to shift for itself, procure at its own risk food and shelter—the most difficult thing in this world. In these painful beginnings it cannot expect any help from its mother, dead some time before; for in insect life the parents generally die before the hatching of the eggs that produce the young. Without delay the little larva sets to work. It eats. It is its sole business, and a serious one, on which its future depends. It eats, not only to keep up its strength from day to day, but above all to acquire the plumpness necessary for its future metamorphosis. I must tell you—and this

"Early stages of the goatweed butterfly" (as well as the other image in this chapter). Illustrations by unknown artist in *The Butterfly Book* by William J. Holland (New York: Doubleday & McClure Co., 1898).

perhaps will surprise you—that an insect ceases to grow after attaining its final perfect form. It is known, too, that there are insects—among others, the butterfly of the silkworm—that do not take any nourishment at all.

"A cat is at first a tiny little pink-nosed creature, so small that it could rest in the hollow of the hand. In one or two months it is a pretty kitten that amuses itself at a mere nothing, and with its nimble paw whips the wisp of paper that one throws before it. Another year, and it is a tom-cat that patiently watches for mice or joins battle with its rivals on the roof. But, whether a tiny creature hardly able to open its little blue eyes, or a pretty playful kitten, or a big quarrelsome tom-cat, it has always the form of a cat.

"It is otherwise with insects. The swallow-tail, under its form of butterfly, is not first small, then medium, then large. When, for the first time, it opens its wings and takes flight, it is as large as it ever will be. When it comes out from under ground, where it lived as a grub, when for the first time it appears in the daylight, the June bug is such as you know it. There are little cats, but no little swallow-tails nor little June bugs. After the metamorphosis, an insect is what it will be to the end."

"But I have seen small June bugs flying round the willows in the evening," objected Jules.

"Those little June bugs are of a different kind. They will always remain the same. Never will they grow and become common June bugs, any more than a cat would grow into a tiger, which it resembles so much.

"The grub alone grows. At first very small on coming out of the egg, little by little it acquires a size in conformity with the future insect. It gathers the materials that the metamorphosis will use,—materials for the wings, antenna, legs, and all those things that the larva does not have, but that the insect must have. Out of what will the big green worm that lives in dead wood, and must someday become a stag-beetle, make the enormous branched mandibles and the robust horny covering of the perfect insect? Of what will the larva make the long antennae of the capricorn? Of what will the caterpillar make the large wings of the swallow-tail? Of that which the caterpillar, larva, and worm amass now, with thrifty hoarding of life-supporting matter.

"If the little pink-nosed cat were born without ears, paws, tail, fur, mustaches, if it were simply a little ball of flesh, and should some day have to acquire all at once, while asleep, ears, paws, tail, fur, mustaches, and many other things, is it not true that this work of life would necessitate materials gathered together beforehand and held in reserve in the fatty tissues of the animal! No thing can be made from nothing; the smallest hair of the cat's mustache shoots forth at the expense of the substance of the animal, substance which it acquires by eating.

"The larva is in precisely this case: it has nothing, or next to nothing, that the perfect insects must have. It must therefore amass, in view of future changes, materials for the change; it must eat for two: for itself first, and then for the insect that will come from its substance, transformed and, in a sense, recast. So the larvae are endowed with an incomparable appetite. As I have said, to eat is their sole business. They eat night and day, often without stopping, without taking breath. To lose a mouthful, what imprudence! The future butterfly would perhaps have one scale less to its wings. So they eat gluttonously, take on a stomach, become big, fat, plump. It is the duty of larvae.

"Some attack plants; they browse on the leaves, chew the flowers, bite the flesh of fruit. Others have a stomach strong enough to digest wood; they hollow out galleries in the tree-trunks, file off, grate, pulverize the hardest oak, as well as the tender willow. Others, again, prefer decomposed animal matter; they haunt infected corpses, fill their stomachs with rottenness. Still others seek excrement and feast on filth. They are all scavengers on whom has developed the high mission of cleansing the earth of its pollution. You would sicken at the mere thought of these worms that swarm in pus; yet one of the most important services, a providential service, is rendered by these disgusting eaters which clear away infection and give back its constituent elements to life. As if to make amends for its filthy needs, one of these larvae will later be a magnificent fly, rivaling polished bronze in its brilliancy; another, a beetle perfumed with musk, its rich coat vying with gold and precious stones in splendor.

"But these larvae devoted to the work of general sanitation cannot make us forget other eaters, of whom we are victims. The grubs of the June bug alone sometimes multiply so rapidly in the ground that immense tracts are denuded of vegetation, which is gnawed at the roots. The forester's shrubs, the farmer's harvests, the gardener's plants, just when everything seems prosperous, some fine morning, hang withered, smitten to death. The worm has passed that way, and all is lost. Fire could not have committed more frightful ravages. A miserable yellow louse, hardly visible, lives under ground, where it attacks the roots of the grape vine. It is called *phylloxera*. Its calamitous breed threatens to destroy all our vineyards. Some grubs, small enough to lodge in a grain of wheat, ravage the wheat in our granaries and leave only the bran. Others browse the lucerne so that the mower finds nothing left. Others, for years, gnaw at the heart of the wood of the oak, poplar, pine, and diverse, other large trees. Others, which turn into those little white butterflies flying around the lamp in the evening and called moths, eat our cloth stuffs bit by bit, and finish by reducing them to rags. Others attack wainscoting, old furniture, and reduce them to powder. Others—But I should never get through if I were to tell you all. This little people, to which we often disdain to pay the slightest attention, this little race of insects, is so powerful on account of the robust appetite of its larvae, that man ought seriously to reckon with it. If a certain grub succeeds in multiplying beyond measure, whole provinces are threatened with the tragic fate of starvation. And we are left in perfect ignorance on the subject of these devourers! How can you defend yourself if the enemy is unknown to you? Ah, if I only had the management of these things! As for you, my dear children, while waiting for our talks to be resumed with more detail concerning these ravagers, remember this: the larvae of insects are the great eaters of this world, the providential demolishers that finish the work of death and thus prepare for the work of life, since everything, or nearly everything passes through their stomach."

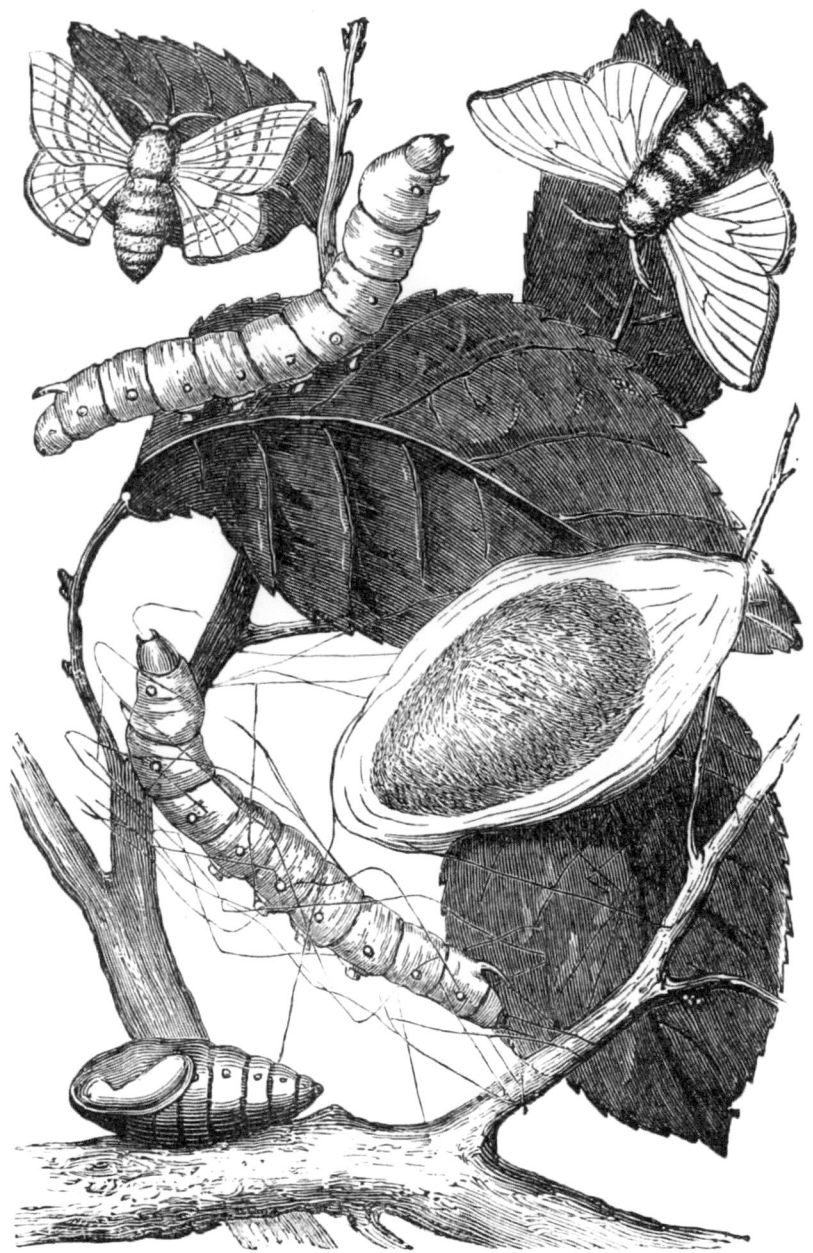

"Larva, pupa, cocoon, and moth of silk-worm." Illustration by unknown artist from *The Popular Science Monthly,* Vol. III. No. 17 (New York: Popular Science Pub. Co., etc. July, 1873).

Week Fifteen:
Silk

"Sooner or later, according to its species, a day comes when the larva feels itself strong enough to face the perils of metamorphosis. It has valiantly done its duty, since to stuff its paunch is the duty of a worm; it has eaten for two, itself and the matured insect. Now it is advisable to renounce feasting, retire from the world, and prepare itself a quiet shelter for the death-like sleep during which its second birth takes place. A thousand methods are employed for the preparation of this lodging.

"Certain larvae simply bury themselves in the ground, others hollow out round niches with polished sides. There are some that make themselves a case out of dry leaves; there are others that know how to glue together a hollow ball out of grains of sand or rotten wood or loam. Those that live in tree-trunks stop up with plugs of sawdust both ends of the galleries they have hollowed out; those that live in wheat gnaw all the farinaceous [filled with starch] part of the gain, scrupulously leaving untouched the outside, or bran, which is to serve them as cradle. Others, with less precaution, shelter themselves in some crack of the bark or of a wall, and fasten themselves there by a string which goes round their body. To this number belong the caterpillars of the cabbage butterfly and the swallow tail. But especially in the making of the silk cell called cocoon is the highest skill of the larvae shown.

"An ashy white caterpillar, the size of the little finger, is raised in large numbers for its cocoon, with which silk stuffs are made. It is called the silkworm. In very clean rooms are placed reed screens, on which they put mulberry leaves, and the young caterpillars come from eggs hatched in the house. The mulberry is a large tree cultivated on purpose to nourish these caterpillars; it has no value except for its leaves, the sole food of silkworms. Large tracts are devoted to its cultivation, so precious is the handiwork of the worm. The caterpillars eat the ration of leaves that is frequently renewed on the screens, and from time to time change their skin, according to their rate of growth. Their appetite is such that the clicking of their jaws is like the noise of a shower falling during a calm on the foliage of the trees. It is true that the room contains thousands and thousands of worms. The caterpillar gets its growth in four or five weeks. Then the screens are set with sprigs of heather, on which the worms climb when the time comes for them to spin their cocoons. They settle themselves one by one amid the sprigs and fasten here and there a multitude of very fine threads, so as to make a kind of network which will hold them suspended and serve them as scaffolding for the great work of the cocoon.

"The silk thread comes out of the under lip, through a hole called the spinneret. In the body of the caterpillar the silk material is a very thick, sticky liquid, resembling gum. In coming through the opening of the lip, this liquid is drawn out into a thread, which glues itself to the preceding threads and immediately hardens. The silk matter is not entirely contained in the mulberry leaf that the worm eats, any more than is milk in the grass that the cow browses. The caterpillar makes it out of the materials of its food, just as the cow makes milk of the constituents of her forage. Without the caterpillar's help man could never extract from the mulberry leaves the material for his costliest fabrics. Our most beautiful silk stuffs really take birth in the worm that drivels them into a thread.

"Let us return to the caterpillar suspended in the midst of its net. Now it is working at the cocoon. Its head is in continual motion. It advances, retires, ascends, descends, goes to right and left, while letting escape from its lip a tiny thread, which rolls itself loosely around the animal, sticks itself to the thread already in place, and finishes by forming a continuous envelope the size of a pigeon's egg. The silken structure is at first transparent enough to permit one to see the caterpillar at work; but as it grows thicker what passes within is soon hidden from view. What follows can easily be guessed. For three or four days the caterpillar continues to thicken the walls of the cocoon until it has exhausted its store of liquid silk. Here it is at last, retired from the world, isolated, tranquil, ready for the transfiguration so soon to take place. Its whole life, its long life of a month, it has worked in anticipation of the metamorphosis; it has crammed itself with mulberry leaves, has extenuated itself to make the silk for its cocoon, but thus it is going to become a butterfly. What a solemn moment for the caterpillar!

"Ah! my children, I had almost forgotten man's part in all this. Hardly is the work of the cocoon finished when he runs to the heather sprig, lays violent hands on the cocoons and sells them to the manufacturer. The latter, without delay, puts them into an oven and subjects them to the action of burning vapor to kill the future butterfly, whose tender flesh is beginning to form. If he delayed, the butterfly would pierce the cocoon, which, no longer capable of being unwound on account of its broken threads, would lose its value. This precaution taken, the rest is done at leisure. The cocoons are unwound in factories called spinning mills. They are put into a pan of boiling water to dissolve the gum which holds the successive windings together. A work-woman armed with a little heather broom stirs them in the water, in order to find and seize the end of the thread, which she puts on a revolving reel. Under the action of the machine the thread of silk unwinds while the cocoon jumps about in the hot water like a ball of wool when one pulls the yam.

"In the center of the threadbare cocoon is the chrysalis, scorched and killed by the fire. Later the silk undergoes diverse operations which give it more suppleness and luster; it passes into the dyer's vats where it takes any color desired; finally it is woven and converted into fabric."

STAGES OF THE SILK MOTH

Egg and first age, lasting five days (an age is the interval between two moultings).

Second age, lasting six days.

Third age, lasting six days.

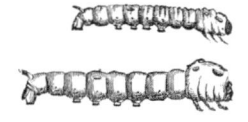

Fourth age, lasting six days.

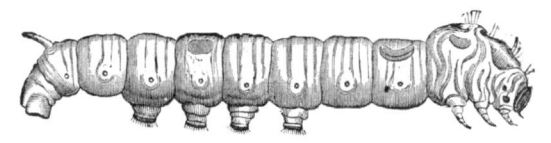

Fifth age, lasting nine days. The mature worm near the end of its career, and at the time of its greatest voracity.

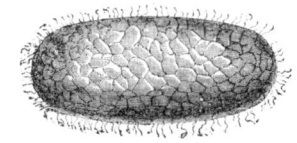

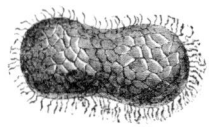

"Spherical cocoon of Bombyx Mori, and cocoon drawn in toward the middle." Illustrations this page by unknown artist in *The Popular Science Monthly,* Vol. III, No. 17 (New York: Popular Science Publishing Co.,1873).

Week Sixteen:
The Metamorphosis

"Once enclosed in its cocoon, the caterpillar withers and shrivels up, as if dying. First, the skin splits on the back; then, by repeated convulsions that pull it this way and that, the worm with much difficulty tears off its skin. With the skin comes everything: the case of the skull, jaws, eyes, legs, stomach and the rest. It is a general tearing-off. The ragged covering of the old body is finally pushed into a corner of the cocoon.

"What do they find then in the cells of silk? Another caterpillar, a butterfly? Neither. They find an almond shaped body, rounded at one end, pointed at the other, of a leathery appearance, and called a chrysalis. It is an intermediate state between the caterpillar and the butterfly. There can be seen certain projections which already indicate the shape of the future insect: at the large end can be distinguished the antennae and the wings tightly folded crosswise on the chrysalis.

"The larvae of the June bug, capricorn, stagbeetle, and other beetles pass through a similar state, but with more accentuated forms. The different parts of the head, wings, legs delicately folded at their sides, are very recognizable. But all is immobile, soft, white, or even transparent as crystal.

This insect in outline is called a nymph. The name of chrysalis used for butterflies and that of nymph used for the other insects signify the same thing under somewhat different appearances. Both the chrysalis and the nymph are insects in process of formation—insects closely wrapped in swaddling clothes, under which is finished the mysterious operation that will change their first structure from top to bottom.

"In a couple of weeks, if the temperature is favorable, the chrysalis of the silkworm opens like a ripe fruit, and from its burst shell the butterfly escapes, all ragged, moist, scarcely able to stand on its trembling legs. Open air is necessary for it to gain strength, to spread and dry its wings. It must get out of the cocoon. But how? The caterpillar has made the cocoon so solid and the butterfly is so weak! Will it perish in its prison, the poor little thing? It would not be worth the trouble of going through so much to stifle miserably in the close cell, just as the end is attained!"

"Could it not tear the cocoon open with its teeth?" asked Emile.

"But, my innocent child, it has none, nor anything like them. It has only a proboscis, incapable of the slightest effort."

"With its claws then?" suggested Jules.

"Yes, if it had any strong enough. The trouble is, it is not provided with any."

"But it must be able to get out," persisted Jules.

"Doubtless it will get out. Has not every creature resources in the difficult moments of life! To break the hen's egg that imprisons it, the tiny little chicken has at the end of its beak a little hard point made on purpose; and the butterfly is to have nothing to open its cocoon? Oh, yes! But you would never guess the singular tool that it will use. It will use its eyes—"

"Its eyes?" interrupted Claire in amazement.

"Yes. Insects' eyes are covered with a cap of transparent horn, hard and cut in facets. A magnifying glass is needed in order to distinguish these facets, they are so fine; but, fine as they are, they have sharp bones which all together can, in time of need, be used as a grater. The butterfly begins then by moistening with a drop of saliva the point of the cocoon it wishes to attack, and then, applying an eye to the spot thus softened, it writhes, knocks, scratches, files. One by one the threads of silk succumb to the rasping. The hole is made, the butterfly comes out. What do you think about it? Do not animals sometimes have intelligence enough for four? Which of us would have thought of forcing the prison walls by striking them with the eye?"

"The butterfly must have studied a long time to think of that ingenious way?" queried Emile.

"The butterfly does not study, does not reflect; it knows at once what to do and how to do well whatever concerns it. Another has reflected for it."

"Who?"

"God himself! God, the great wise one. The silkworm butterfly is not pretty. It is whitish, tun-bellied, heavy. It does not fly like the others from flower to flower, for it takes no nourishment. As soon as it is out of the cocoon, it sets to work laying eggs; then it dies. Silkworm eggs are commonly called seed, a very good term, for the egg is the seed of the animal as the seed is the egg of the plant. Egg and seed correspond. They do not stifle all the cocoons in the vapor to wind them afterwards; they keep out a certain number so as to obtain butterflies and consequently eggs or seeds. These are the seeds which, the following year, produce the fresh brood of worms.

"All insects that are metamorphosed pass through the four states that I have just told you about: egg, larva, chrysalis or nymph, perfect insect. The perfect insect lays its eggs, and the series of transformations begins again."

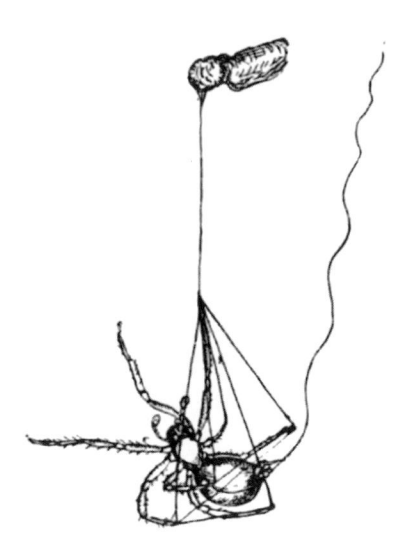

"The swinging basket used in issuing trial cables," Illustration by unknown artist in *American Spiders and Their Spinning Work* by Henry C. McCook (Philadelphia: Academy of Natural Sciences of Philadelphia. c. 1889–1893).

Week Seventeen:
Spiders

ONE morning, Mother Ambroisine was chopping herbs and cooked apples for a brood of little chickens hatched not long before. A large gray spider, letting itself slide the length of its thread, descended from the ceiling to the good woman's shoulders. At sight of the creature with long, velvety legs, Mother Ambroisine could not suppress a cry of fear, and, shaking her shoulder, made the insect fall, and crushed it under her foot. "Spider in the morning stands for mourning," said she to herself. At this instant Uncle Paul and Claire entered.

"No, sir, it is not right," said Mother Ambroisine, "That we poor mortals should have so much useless trouble. Twelve little chickens are hatched out for us, bright as gold; and just as I am preparing them something to eat, a villainous spider falls on my shoulder."

And Mother Ambroisine pointed with her finger at the crushed insect with its legs still trembling.

"I do not see that those little chickens have anything to fear from the spider," remarked Uncle Paul.

"Oh! nothing, sir: the horrid creature is dead. But you know the proverb: 'Spider in the morning, mourning; spider at night, delight.' Everybody knows that a spider seen in the morning is a sign of bad luck. Our little chickens are in danger; the cats will claw them. You'll see, sir, you'll see."

Tears of emotion came to Mother Ambroisine's eyes.

"Put the little chickens in a safe place, watch the cats, and I will answer for the rest. The proverb of the spider is only a foolish prejudice," said Uncle Paul.

Mother Ambroisine did not utter another word. She knew that Maître Paul found a reason for everything, and on occasion was capable of pronouncing a eulogy on the spider. Claire, who saw this eulogy coming, ventured a question.

"I know, in your eyes all animals, however hideous they may be, have excellent excuses to plead: all merit consideration; all play a part ordained by Providence; all are interesting to observe and to study. You are the advocate of the good God's creatures; you would plead for the toad. But permit your niece to see there only an impulse of your kind heart, and not the real truth. What could you say in praise of the spider, horrid beast, which is poisonous and disfigures the ceiling with its webs!"

"What could I say? Much, my dear child, much. In the meantime, feed your little chickens and beware of cats if you want to prove the spider proverb false."

In the evening Mother Ambroisine, her round spectacles, on her nose, was knitting stockings. On her knees the cat slept and mingled its purring with the tick-tack of the needles. The children were waiting for the story of the spider. Their uncle began.

"Which of you three can tell me what spiders do with their webs, those fine webs stretched in the corners of the granary or between two shrubs in the garden?"

Emile spoke first. "It is their nest, Uncle, their house, their hiding-place."

"Hiding-place!" exclaimed Jules; "yes, I think it is more than that. One day I heard, between the lilac branches, a little shrill noise—he-e-e-e! A blue fly was entangled in a cobweb and trying to escape. It was the fly that was making the noise with its fluttering. A spider ran from the bottom of the silken funnel, seized the fly, and carried it off to its hole, doubtless to eat it. Since then I have thought spiders' webs were hunting nets."

"That is even so," said his uncle. "All spiders live on live prey; they make continual war on flies, gnats, and other insects. If you fear mosquitoes, those insufferable little insects that sting us at night until they bring blood, you must bless the spider, for it does its best to rid us of them. To catch game, a net is necessary. Now, the net to catch flies in their flight is a cloth woven with silk, which the spider itself produces.

"In the body of the insect the silky matter is, as with caterpillars, a sticky liquid resembling glue or gum. As soon as it comes in contact with the air, this matter congeals, hardens, and becomes a thread on which water has no effect. When the spider wants to spin, the silk liquid flows from four nipples, called spinnerets, placed at the end of the stomach. These nipples are pierced at their extremity by a number of holes, like the sprinkler of a watering-pot. The number of these holes for all the nipples is roughly reckoned as a thousand. Each one lets its tiny little jet of liquid flow, which hardens and becomes thread; and from a thousand threads stuck together into one results the final thread employed by the spider. To designate something very fine there is no better term of comparison than the spider's thread. It is so delicate, in fact, that it can only just be seen. Our silk threads, those of the finest textures, are cables in comparison, cables of two, three, four strands, while this one, in its unequaled tenuity, contains a thousand. How many spiders' threads are required to make a strand of the thickness of a hair? Not far from ten. And how many elementary threads, such as issue from the separate holes of the spinneret? Ten thousand. To what a degree of tenuity then this silky matter can be reduced that stretches out in threads of which it takes ten thousand to equal the size of one hair! What marvels, my children, and only to catch a fly that is to serve for the spider's dinner!"

"Spider Suspension Bridge Over a Stream." Illustration by unknown artist in *American Spiders and Their Spinning Work* by Henry C. McCook (Philadelphia: Academy of Natural Sciences of Philadelphia. c. 1889–1893).

Week Eighteen:
The Epeira's Bridge

HERE Uncle Paul caught Claire looking at him thoughtfully. It was evident that some change was taking place in her mind: the spider was no longer a repulsive creature, unworthy of our regard. Uncle Paul continued:

"With its legs, armed with sharp-toothed little claws like combs, the spider draws the thread from its spinnerets as it has need. If it wishes to descend, like the one this morning that came down from the ceiling on to Mother Ambroisine's shoulder, it glues the end of the thread to the point of departure and lets itself fall perpendicularly. The thread is drawn from the spinnerets by the weight of the spider, and the latter, softly suspended, descends to any depth it wishes, and as slowly as it pleases. In order to ascend again, it climbs up the thread by folding it gradually into a skein between its legs. For a second descent, the spider has only to let its skein of silk unwind little by little.

"To weave its web, each kind of spider has its own method of procedure, according to the kind of game it is going to hunt, the places it frequents, and according to its particular inclinations, tastes, and instincts. I will merely tell you a few words about the *Epeiræ*, large spiders magnificently speckled with yellow, black, and silvery white. They are hunters of big game,—of green or blue damsel-flies that frequent the water-courses, of butterflies, and large flies. They stretch their web vertically between two trees and even from one bank of a stream to the other. Let us examine this last case.

"An epeira has found a good place for hunting: the dragon-flies, or blue and green damsel-flies, come and go from one tuft of reeds to another, sometimes going up, sometimes down the stream. Along its course are butterflies also, and horse-flies, or large flies that suck blood from cattle. The site is a good one. Now, then, to work! The epeira climbs to the top of a willow at the water's edge. There it matures its plan, an audacious one, the execution of which seems impossible. A suspension bridge, a cable which serves as support for the future web, must be stretched from one bank to the other. And observe, children, that the spider cannot cross the stream by swimming; it would perish by drowning if it ventured into the water. It must stretch its cable, its bridge, from the top of its branch without changing place. Never has an engineer found himself in such difficulties. What will the little creature do? Put your heads together, children; I am waiting for your ideas."

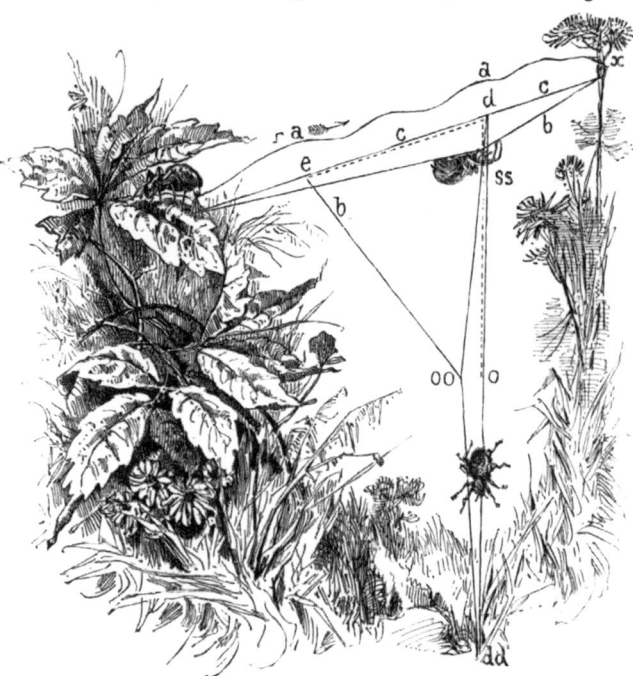

"Laying foundation lines by air currents (first lines)." Illustration by unknown artist in *American Spiders and Their Spinning Work* by Henry C. McCook (Philadelphia: Academy of Natural Sciences of Philadelphia. c. 1889–1893).

THE EPEIRA'S BRIDGE

"Build a bridge from one side to the other, without crossing the water or moving away from its place! If the spider can do that it is cleverer than I am." Thus spoke Jules.

"Than I, too," chimed in his brother.

"If I did not already know," said Claire, "since you have just told us, that the spider does accomplish it, I should say that its bridge is impossible."

Mother Ambroisine said nothing, but by the slackening of the tick-tack of her needles, every one could see that she was much interested in the spider's bridge.

"Animals often have more intelligence than we," continued Uncle Paul; "the epeira will prove it to us. With its hind legs it draws a thread from its spinnerets. The thread lengthens and lengthens; it floats from the top of the branch. The spider draws out more and more; finally, it stops. Is the thread long enough? Is it too short? That is what must be looked after. If too long, it would be wasting the precious silky liquid; if too short, it would not fulfill the given conditions. A glance is thrown at the distance to be crossed, an exact glance, you may be sure. The thread is found too short. The spider lengthens it by drawing out a little more. Now all goes well: the thread has the wished-for length, and the work is done. The epeira waits at the top of its branch: the rest will be accomplished without help. From time to time it bears with its legs on the thread to see if it resists. Ah! it resists; the bridge is fixed! The spider crosses the stream on its suspension bridge! What has happened, then? This: The thread floated from the top of the willow. A breath of air blew the free end of the thread into the branches on the opposite

"Young spider preparing for an aerial voyage." Illustration by unknown artist in *Spiders* by Cecil Warburton (Cambridge: University Press. 1912).

bank. This end got entangled there; behold the mystery. The epeira has only to draw the thread to itself, to stretch it properly and make a suspension bridge of it."

"Oh, how simple!" cried Jules. "And yet not one of us would have thought of it."

"Yes, my friend, it is very simple, but at the same time very ingenious. It is thus with all work: simplicity in the means employed is a sign of excellence. To simplify is to have knowledge; to complicate is to be ignorant. The epeira, in its kind of construction, is science perfected."

"Where does it get that science, Uncle?" asked Claire. "Animals have not reason. Then who teaches the epeira to build its suspension bridges?"

"No one, my dear child; it is born with this knowledge. It has it by instinct, the infallible inspiration of the Father of all things, who creates in the least of His creatures, for their preservation, ways of acting before which our reason is often confounded. When the epeira, from the top of the willow, gets ready to spin its web, what inspires it with the audacious project of the bridge; what gives it patience to wait for the floating end of the thread to entwine in the branches of the other bank; what assures it of the success of a labor that it is performing perhaps for the first time, and has never seen done? It is the universal Reason that watches over creation, and takes among men the thrice-holy name of Providence."

Uncle Paul had won his case: in the eyes of all, even of Mother Ambroisine, spiders were no longer frightful creatures.

Week Nineteen:
The Spider's Web

THE next day the little chickens were all hatched and doing well. The hen had led them to the courtyard, and, scratching the soil and clucking, she dug up small seeds which the little ones came and took from their mother's beak. At the slightest approach of danger, the hen called the brood, and all ran to snuggle under her outspread wings. The boldest soon put their heads out, their pretty little yellow heads framed in their mother's black feathers. The alarm over, the hen began clucking and scratching again, and the little ones went trotting around her once more. Completely reassured, Mother Ambroisine forever renounced her proverb of the spider. In the evening Uncle Paul continued the story of the epeira.

"Since it must serve as a support to the silken network, the first thread stretched from one bank to the other must be of exceptional firmness. The epeira begins, therefore, by fixing both ends well; then, going and coming on the thread from one extremity to the other, always spinning, it doubles and trebles the strands and sticks them together in a common cable. A second similar cable is necessary, placed beneath the first in an almost parallel direction. It is between the two that the web must be spun.

"For this purpose, from one of the ends of the cable already constructed the epeira lets itself fall perpendicularly, hanging by the thread that escapes from its spinnerets. It reaches a lower branch, fastens the thread firmly to it, and ascends to the communicating bridge by the vertical thread it used for descending. The spider then reaches the other bank, still spinning, but without gluing this new strand of silk to the cable. Arrived at the other side, it lets itself slide on to a branch conveniently placed, and there fastens the end of the thread that it has spun on its way from one bank to the other. This second chief piece of the framework becomes a cable by the addition of new threads. Finally, the two parallel cables are made firm at each end by diverse threads starting from it in every direction and attaching themselves to the branches. Other threads go out from this point and that, from one cable to the other, leaving between them, in the middle of the construction, a large open space, almost circular, destined for the net.

"Epeira moving with dragline and anchorage."
Illustration by unknown artist in *American Spiders and Their Spinning Work* by Henry C. McCook (Philadelphia: Academy of Natural Sciences of Philadelphia. c. 1889–1893).

"Thus far the epeira has only constructed the framework of its building, a rough but solid framework; now begins the work of fine precision. The net must be spun. Across the open circular space that the diverse threads of the framework leave between them, a first thread is stretched. The epeira stations itself right in the middle of this thread, central point of the web to be constructed. From this center numerous threads must start at equal distances from one another and be fastened to the circumference by the other end. They are called radiating lines. Accordingly the epeira glues a thread to the center and, ascending by the transverse thread already stretched, fixes the end of the line to the circumference. That done, it returns to the center by the line that it has just stretched; there it glues a second thread and immediately regains the circumference, where it fastens the end of the second line a short distance from the first one. Going thus alternately from the center to the circumference and from the circumference to the center by way of the last thread just stretched, the spider fills the circular space with radiating lines so regularly spaced that you would say they were traced with rule and compass by an expert hand.

"When the radiating lines are finished, the most delicate work of all is still left for the spider. Each of these lines must be bound by a thread that, starting at the circumference, twists and turns in a spiral line around the center, where it terminates. The epeira starts from the top of the web and, unwinding its thread, stretches it from one radiating line to another, keeping always at an equal distance from the outside thread. By thus circling about, always at the same distance from the preceding thread, the spider ends at the center of the radiating lines. The network is then finished.

"Now there must be arranged a little ambuscade [ambush] from which the epeira can survey its web, a resting room where it finds shelter from the coolness of the night and the heat of the day. In a little bunch of leaves close together the spider builds itself a silk den, a sort of funnel of close texture. That is its usual abiding place. If the weather is favorable and the passage of game abundant, morning and evening especially, the epeira leaves its den and posts itself, motionless, in the center of the web, to watch events more closely and run to the game quickly enough to prevent its escape. The spider is at its post, in the middle of the network, its eight legs spread out wide. It does not move, pretends to be dead. No hunter on the watch would have such patience. Let us copy its example and await the coming of the game."

The children were disappointed: at the moment when the story became the most interesting, Uncle Paul broke off his narrative.

"The epeira has interested me very much. Uncle," said Jules. "The bridge over the stream, the cobweb with its regular radiating lines, and the thread that twists and turns, getting nearer and nearer to the center, the room for ambush and rest—all that is very astonishing in a creature that does these wonderful things without having to learn how. Catching the game ought to be still more curious."

"Very curious indeed. Therefore, instead of telling you about the hunt, I prefer to show it to you. Yesterday, in crossing the field, I saw an epeira constructing its web between two trees on the little stream where such fine crayfish are caught. Let us get up early in the morning and go and see the chase."

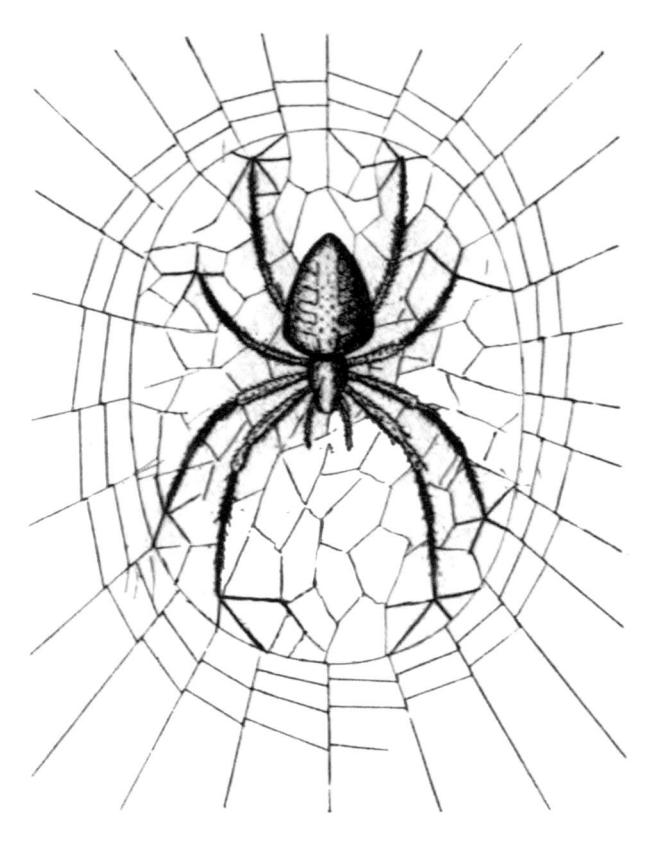

"Position of Epeira upon her Hub, to show command of the snare." Illustration by unknown artist in *American Spiders and Their Spinning Work* by Henry C. McCook (Philadelphia: Academy of Natural Sciences of Philadelphia. c. 1889–1893).

Week Twenty:
The Chase

UNCLE PAUL had said: "Let us get up early in the morning." No one had to be called. One sleeps little when one is going to see an epeira hunt. About seven o'clock, with the sun shining bright, they were at the border of the stream. The cobweb was finished. Some dewdrops hanging to the threads shone like pearls. Hence the spider was not yet in the center of the net; no doubt it was waiting, before descending from its room, for the sun to dissipate the morning dampness. The party sat down on the grass for breakfast, at the very foot of the alder-tree to which were fastened the cables of the net. Blue damsel-flies flew from one tuft of rushes to another and chased each other playfully. Beware, you giddy ones, who will not know how to avoid the web by passing over and under it! Ah! It has happened; so much the worse for the victim. When one plays foolishly with one's companions, one must at least look where one is going. A dragon-fly is caught in the meshes of the web. With one wing free it struggles to escape. It shakes the web, but the cables hold in spite of the shaking. Threads in communication with the resting-room warn the epeira, by their agitation, of the important things taking place in the net. The spider hastily descends, but it does not get there in time. With a desperate stroke of its wing the dragon-fly frees itself and escapes, tearing a large hole in the web.

"Oh! how well it got out!" cried Jules. "A little more and the poor thing would have been eaten alive. Did you see, Emile, how quickly the spider ran down from its hiding place when it felt the web move! The hunt begins badly; the game escapes and the net is torn."

"Yes, but the spider is going to mend it," his uncle reassured him.

And, in fact, as soon as it had recovered from its misadventure, the epeira renewed the broken threads with delicate dexterity. The darning finished, the damage could hardly be detected. The spider now takes its place in the center of the network: the right moment for the chase has come, apparently, and it is advisable for it to pounce upon the game as quickly as possible, to avoid other misadventures. It spreads its eight feet in a circle, to receive the slightest movement that may come at any point of the web, and it waits, completely motionless.

The dragon-flies continue their evolutions. Not one is caught: the recent alarm has rendered them circumspect; they fly around the web to pass beyond it. Oh! oh! What is that coming so giddily and striking its head against the network? It is a little bumble-bee, all velvety and black, with a red stomach. It is caught. The epeira runs. But the captive is vigorous and formidable; perhaps it has a sting. The spider mistrusts it. It draws a thread from its spinneret and passes it quickly over the bee. A second silk string, a third, a fourth, soon subdue the captive's desperate efforts. Here is the bee strangled but still full of life, and menacing. To seize it in that state would be great imprudence: the epeira's life would be at stake. What must be done so as to leave nothing to fear from this dangerous prey? The spider possesses, folded under its head, two sharp-pointed fangs, which let flow a little drop of poison through a hole in their extremities. That is its hunting weapon. The epeira approaches cautiously, opens its fangs, stings the bee, and immediately moves aside. In the twinkling of an eye it is all over. The poison acts instantly: the bee trembles, its legs stiffen, it is dead. The spider carries it off to its silken chamber to suck it at leisure. When nothing but the skin is left, the spider will throw the remains of the bee far from its domicile, so as not to soil its web with a corpse that might frighten other game.

"It was done so quickly," complained Jules, "I did not see the spider's poisonous fangs. If we were to wait a little longer, another bumble-bee might perhaps come and then I should see it better."

"It is not necessary to wait," replied Uncle Paul. "If we proceed skilfully we can make the spider recommence its hunting maneuvers. All of you look attentively."

Uncle Paul searched among the field flowers for a moment and caught a large fly; then, holding it by one wing, put it near the web. The insect, beating about, gets entangled in the threads. The web shakes, the spider leaves its bee and runs, delighted with the fortunate chance that brings him prey again so quickly. The same maneuvers begin again. The fly is first strangled; the epeira opens its pointed fangs, stings the fly a little, and all is over. The victim trembles, stretches itself out, and ceases to move.

"Ah! that time I saw it," said Jules, satisfied at last.

"Claire, did you notice the fineness of the spider's fangs?" asked Emile. "I am sure that in your needle-case you haven't any such fine-pointed needles."

"I dare say not. As for me, what surprises me the most is not the fineness of the spider's fangs, but the quickness of the victim's death. It seems to me that a fly as large as this one ought not to die so quickly even from the coarser pricks of our needles."

"Very true," assented her uncle. "An insect transfixed by a pin still lives a long time; but if it is only pricked by the fine point of the spider's fangs it dies almost instantly. But then, the spider takes care to poison its weapon. Its fangs are venomous; they are perforated by a minute canal through which the spider lets flow at will a scarcely visible little drop of liquid called venom, which the creature makes as it makes the silk liquid. The venom is held in reserve in a slender pocket placed in the interior of the fangs. When the spider pricks its prey, it makes a little of this liquid pass into the wound, and that suffices to bring speedy death to the wounded insect. The victim dies, not from the prick itself, but from the dreadful ravages wrought by the venom discharged into the wound."

Here Uncle Paul, in order to give his hearers a better view of the poisonous fangs, took the epeira with the tips of his fingers. Claire uttered a cry of fear, but her uncle soon calmed her.

"Don't be uneasy, my dear child: the poison that kills a fly will have no effect on Uncle Paul's hard skin."

And with the aid of a pin he opened the creature's fangs to show them in detail to the children, who were quite reassured.

"You must not be too frightened," he continued, "at the quick death of the fly and of the bumble-bee, and so look on spiders as creatures to be feared by us. The fangs of most of them would have great difficulty in piercing our skin. Courageous observers have let themselves be bitten by the various spiders of our country. The sting has never produced any serious results; nothing more than a redness less painful than that produced by the sting of a mosquito. At the same time, persons with a delicate skin ought to beware of the large kinds, were it only to spare themselves a passing pain. Without any excessive alarm we avoid the wasp's sting, which is very painful; let us avoid the spider's fangs in the same way without uttering loud cries at the sight of one of these creatures. We will resume the subject of the venomous insects. But it is late; let us go."

Week Twenty-one:
Venomous Insects

"YOU have heard that certain creatures emit poison, that is to say, shoot from a distance into the face and on to the hands of those who approach, a liquid capable of causing death, or at least of blinding or otherwise injuring them. Last week Jules found on the leaves of the potato-vines a large caterpillar armed with a curved horn."

"I know, I know," put in Jules. "It is the caterpillar, you told me, that turns into a magnificent butterfly called the *Sphinx Atropos*. This butterfly, large as my hand, has on its back a white spot that frightens many people, for it has a vague resemblance to a death's-head moth. And besides, its eyes shine in the dark. You added that it was a harmless creature of which it would be unreasonable to be afraid."

"Jacques, who was weeding the potatoes," continued Uncle Paul, "knocked the sphinx caterpillar out of Jules's hands, and hastened to crush it with his big wooden shoe. 'What you are doing is very dangerous,' said the good Jacques. 'Handling poisonous creatures—of all things! Do you see that green venom! Don't get too close; the silly thing is not quite dead; it might yet throw some poison on you.' The worthy man took the green entrails of the crushed caterpillar for poison. Those entrails did not contain anything dangerous; they were green because they were swollen with the juice of the leaves that the poor thing had just eaten.

"Many persons are of the same opinion as Jacques: they are afraid of a caterpillar and the green of its entrails. They think that certain creatures poison everything they touch and throw out venom. Well, my dear children, you must bear this in mind, for it is a very important thing and frees us from foolish fears, while it puts us on guard against real danger: no animal of any kind, absolutely none, shoots venom and can harm us from a distance. To be convinced of this it suffices to know what venom really is. Diverse creatures, large or small, are endowed with a poisoned weapon that serves them either as defense or to attack their prey. The bee is our best known venomous creature."

"What!" exclaimed Emile, "A bee is poisonous, the bee that makes honey for us?"

"Yes, the bee; the bee without which we could not have those honey cakes that Mother Ambroisine hands round when you are good. You don't think then of the stings that made you cry so!"

Emile blushed: his uncle had just revived unpleasant memories. From pure heedlessness he tried one day to see what the bees were doing. They say he even thrust a stick through the little door of the hive. The bees became incensed at this indiscretion. Three or four stung the poor boy on the cheeks and hands. He cried out most piteously, and thought himself done for. His uncle had much

(ABOVE) "A Swarm of Bees." (OPPOSITE) "The Sting of a Bee." Unknown photographer printed in *Bees, Wasps, and Ants* by F. Martin Duncan and Lucy T. Duncan (London: Henry Frowde: Oxford University Press, 1913)..

difficulty in consoling him. Compresses of cold water finally soothed his smarting pains.

"The bee is venomous," repeated Uncle Paul; "Emile could tell you that!"

"The wasp too, then?" asked Jules. "One stung me once when I tried to drive it from a bunch of grapes. I did not say anything, but all the same I was not very comfortable. To think that such a tiny thing can hurt one so! It seemed as if my hands were on fire."

"Certainly, the wasp is venomous; more so than the bee, in the sense that its sting causes greater pain. Bumble-bees are, too, as well as hornets, those large reddish wasps, an inch long, which sometimes come and gnaw the pears in the orchard. You must beware especially of hornets, my little friends. One sting from them, one only, would give you hours of horrible pain.

"All these insects have, for their defense, a poisoned weapon constructed in the same way. It is called the sting. It is a small, hard, and very pointed blade, a kind of dagger finer than the finest needle placed at the end of the creature's stomach. When in repose, it is not seen; it is hidden in a scabbard that goes into its stomach. To defend itself, the insect draws it out of its sheath and plunges the point into the imprudent finger found within reach.

"Now it is not exactly the wound made by the sting that causes the smarting pain that you are familiar with. This wound is so slight, so minute, we cannot see it. We should hardly feel it were it made with a needle or a thorn as fine as the sting. But the sting communicates with a pocket of venom lodged in the creature's body, and, by means of a hollowed-out canal, it carries to the bottom of the wound a little drop of the formidable liquid. The sting is then drawn back. As to the venom, it stays in the wound, and it is that, that alone, which causes those shooting pains that Emile could, if necessary, tell us about."

At this second attack from Uncle Paul, who dwelt on this misadventure in order to blame him for his heedless treatment of the bees, Emile blew his nose, although he did not need to. It was a way of hiding his confusion. His uncle did not appear to notice it, and continued:

"Scholars who have made a study of this curious question tell us of the following experiment, to make clear that it is really the venomous liquid introduced into the wound, and not the wound itself, that causes the pain. When one pricks oneself with a very fine needle, the hurt is very slight and soon passes off. I am sure Claire is not much frightened when she pricks her finger in sewing."

"Oh! no," said she. "That is so soon over, even if blood comes."

"Well, the prick of a needle, insignificant in itself, can cause sharp pains if the little wound is poisoned with the venom of the bee or wasp. The scholars I am telling you of dip the point of the needle into the bee's pocket of venom, and with this point thus wet with the venomous liquid give themselves a slight sting. The pain is now sharp and of long duration, more so than if the insect itself had stung the experimenter. This increase of pain is due to the fact that the comparatively large needle introduces into the wound more venom than could the bee's slender sting. You understand it now, I hope: it is the introduction of the venom into the wound that causes all the trouble."

"That is plain," said Jules. "But tell me, Uncle, why these scholars amuse themselves by pricking themselves with needles dipped in the bee's venom? It is a queer amusement, to hurt oneself for nothing."

"For nothing, Mr. Harum-scarum? Do you count as nothing what I have just told you? If I know it, must not others have taught me? Who are these others? They are the valiant investigators who learn about everything, observe and study everything, in order to alleviate our suffering. When they voluntarily prick themselves with poison, they propose to study in themselves, at their own risk and peril, the action of the venom, to teach us to combat its effects, which are sometimes so formidable. Let a viper or a scorpion sting us, and our life is in peril. Ah, then it is important to know exactly how the venom acts and what must be done to arrest its ravages; it is then that the scholars' researches are appreciated, researches that Jules looks upon as merely a queer amusement. Science, my little friend, has sacred enthusiasms that do not shrink from any test that may enlarge the sphere of our knowledge and diminish human suffering."

Jules, confused by his unfortunate remark, lowered his head and said not a word. Uncle Paul was on the point of getting vexed, but peace was soon restored, and he continued the account of venomous creatures.

"The wasp's nest is made of a thin, flexible material like brown paper, formed of particles of wood." Illustration by E. J. Detmold in *Fabre's Book of Insects* by Jean-Henri Fabre, translated by Mrs. Rodolph Stawell (New York: Dodd, Mead. c. 1921).

Week Twenty-two:
Venom

ALL venomous creatures act in the same way as the bee, wasp, and hornet. With a special weapon—needle, fang, sting, lancet—placed sometimes in one part of the body, sometimes in another, according to the species, they make a slight wound into which is instilled a drop of venom. The weapon has no other effect than that of opening a route for the venomous liquid, and this is what causes the injury. For the poison to act on us, it must come in contact with our blood by a wound which opens the way for it. But it has positively no effect on our skin, unless there is already a gash, a simple scratch, that permits it to penetrate into the flesh and mingle with the blood. The most terrible venom can be handled without any danger if the skin is not broken. Moreover, it can be put on the lips, on the tongue, even swallowed without any bad results. Placed on the lips, the hornet's venom produces no more effect than clear water; but if there is the slightest scratch the pain is atrocious. The viper's venom is equally harmless as long as it does not mingle with the blood. Courageous

---

This chapter contains outdated information on how to treat a snake bite. It is not recommended that you create a tourniquet or suck out venom. Consider researching with your family the modern recommendations for venom survival!

experimenters have tasted and swallowed it, and yet afterward were no worse off than before."

"Is that true, Uncle? People have had the courage to swallow a viper's venom? Ah! I should not have been so brave." This from Claire.

"It is fortunate, my girl, that others have been so for us; and we ought to be very grateful to them, for by so doing they have taught us, as you will see, the most prompt and one of the most efficacious means to employ in ease of accident."

"This viper's venom, which has no effect on the hand, lips, and tongue, is it much to be feared if it mingles with the blood?"

"It is terrible, my young lady, and I was just going to tell you about it. Let us suppose that some imprudent person disturbs the formidable reptile sleeping in the sun. Suddenly the creature uncoils itself in circles one above another, unwinds with the suddenness of a spring, and, with its jaws wide open, strikes you on the hand. It is done in the twinkling of an eye. With the same rapidity the viper refolds its spiral and draws back, continuing to menace you with its head in the center of the coil. You do not wait for a second attack, you flee; but, alas! the damage is done. On the wounded hand are seen two little red points, almost insignificant, mere needle pricks. It is not very alarming; you reassure yourself if you are in ignorance of what I so earnestly desire to teach you. Delusive innocuousness! See the red spots becoming encircled with a livid ring. With dull pains the hand swells, and the swelling extends gradually to the arm. Soon come cold sweats and nausea; respiration becomes painful, sight troubled, mind torpid, a general yellowness shows itself, accompanied by convulsions. If help does not arrive in time, death may come."

"You give us goose-flesh, Uncle," said Jules, with a shudder. "What should we poor things do if such a misfortune happened to us away from you, away from home? They say there are vipers in the underbrush of the neighboring hills."

"May God guard you from such a mischance, my poor children! But, if it befalls you, you must bind tight the finger, hand, arm, above the wounded part to prevent the diffusion of the venom in the blood;

you must make the wound bleed by pressing round it; you must suck it hard to extract the venomous liquid. I told you venom has no effect on the skin. To suck it, therefore, is harmless if the mouth has no scratch. You can see that if, by hard suction and by pressure that makes the blood flow, you succeed in extracting all the venom from the wound, the wound itself is thenceforth of no importance. For greater surety, the wound should be cauterized as soon as possible with a corrosive liquid, *aqua fortis* or ammonia, or even with a red-hot iron. The effect of the cauterization is to destroy the venomous matter. It is painful, I acknowledge, but one must submit to it in order to avoid a worse evil. Cauterization is the doctor's business. The initial precautions, binding to prevent the diffusion of the venom, pressure to make the poisoned blood flow, hard suction to extract the venomous liquid, concern us personally, and all that must be done instantly. The longer it is put off, the more aggravated the evil. When these precautions are taken soon enough, it is seldom that the viper's bite has injurious consequences."

"You reassure me, Uncle. Those precautions are not difficult to take, if one does not lose one's presence of mind."

"Therefore it is important that we should all acquire the habit of using our reason in time of danger, and not let ourselves be overcome by ill-regulated fears. Man master of himself is half-master of danger."

"Viper, or Adder." Illustration here and on page 144 by unknown artist in *Our Reptiles and Batrachians: a Plain and Easy Account of the Lizards, Snakes, Newts, Toads, Frogs and Tortoises Indigenous to Great Britain* by Mordecai C. Cooke (London: W. H. Allen. 1893).

Week Twenty-three:
The Viper and the Scorpion

"YOU just said," interposed Emile, "the *bite* of the viper, and not the *sting*. Then serpents bite, and do not sting. I thought it was just the other way. I have always heard they had a sting. Last Thursday lame Louis, who is not afraid of anything, caught a serpent in a hole of the old Wall. He had two comrades with him. They bound the creature round the neck with a rush. I was passing, and they called me. The serpent was darting from its mouth something black, pointed, flexible, which came and went rapidly. I thought it was the sting and was much afraid of it. Louis laughed. He said what I took for a sting was the serpent's tongue; and to prove it to me, he put his hand near it."

"Louis was right," replied Uncle Paul. "All serpents dart a very flexible, forked, black filament between their lips with great swiftness. For many purposes it is the reptile's weapon, or dart; but in reality this filament is nothing but the tongue, a quite inoffensive tongue, which the creature uses to catch insects and to express in its peculiar manner the passions that agitate it by darting it quickly from between the lips. All serpents, without any exception, have one; but in our countries the viper alone possesses the terrible venomous apparatus.

"This apparatus is composed, first, of two hooks, or teeth, long and pointed, placed in the upper jaw. At the will of the creature they stand up erect for the attack or lie down in a groove of the gum, and hold themselves there as inoffensive as a stiletto in its sheath. In that way the reptile runs no danger of wounding itself. These fangs are hollow and pierced toward the point by a small opening through which the venom is injected into the wound. Finally, at the base of each fang is a little pocket full of venomous liquid. It is an innocent-looking humor [archaic for fluid, from the Latin *humorem* for moisture] odorless, tasteless; one would almost think it was water. When the viper strikes with its fangs, the venomous pocket drives a drop of its contents into the canal of the tooth, and the terrible liquid is instilled into the wound.

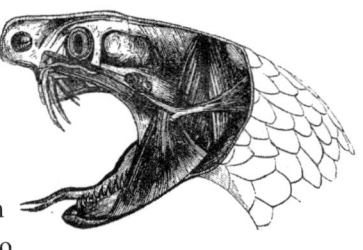

"By preference the viper inhabits warm and rocky hills; it keeps under stones and thickets of brush. It is brown or reddish in color. On the back it has a somber zigzag band, and on each side a row of spots. Its stomach is slate-gray. Its head is a little triangular, larger than the neck, obtuse and as if cut off in front. The viper is timid and fearful; it attacks man only in self-defense. Its movements are brusk, irregular, and sluggish.

"The other serpents of our countries, serpents designated by the general name of snakes, have not the venomous fangs of the viper. Their bite therefore is not of importance, and the repugnance they inspire in us is really groundless.

"Next to the viper there is in France no venomous creature more to be feared than the scorpion. It is very ugly and walks on eight feet. In front it has two pincers like those of the crayfish, and behind a knotty, curled tail ending in a sting. The pincers are inoffensive, despite their menacing aspect; it is the sting with which the end of the tail is armed that is venomous. The scorpion makes use of it in self defense and to kill the insects on which it feeds. In the southern departments of France are found two different kinds of scorpions. One, of a greenish black, frequents dark and cool places and even establishes itself in houses. It leaves its retreat only at night. It can be seen then running on the damp and cracked walls, seeking wood-lice and spiders, its customary prey. The other, much larger, is pale yellow. It keeps under warm and sandy stones. The black scorpion's sting does not cause serious injury; that of the yellow may be mortal. When one of these creatures is irritated, a little drop of liquid can be seen forming into a pearl at the extremity of the sting, which is all ready to strike. It is the drop of venom that the scorpion injects into the wound.

"There are many other important things I could tell you about the venomous creatures of foreign countries, about diverse serpents whose bite causes a dreadful death; but I hear Mother Ambroisine calling us to dinner. Let us go over rapidly what I have just told you. No creature, however ugly it may be, shoots venom or can do us any harm from a distance. All venomous species act in the same way: with a special weapon a slight wound is made; and into this wound a drop of venom is introduced. The wound, by itself, is nothing; it is the injected liquid that makes it painful and sometimes mortal. The venomous weapon serves the creature for hunting and for defense. It is placed in a part of the body that varies according to the species. Spiders have a double fang folded at the entrance of the mouth; bees, wasps, hornets, bumblebees, have a sting at the end of the stomach and kept invisible in its sheath when in repose; the viper and all venomous serpents have two long hollowed-out teeth on the upper jaw; the scorpion carries a sting at the end of its tail."

"I am very sorry," said Jules, "that Jacques did not hear your account of venomous creatures; he would have understood that caterpillars' green entrails are not venom. I will tell him all these things; and if I find another beautiful sphinx caterpillar I will not crush it."

"Sometimes the scarab seems to enter into partnership with a friend." Illustration by E. J. Detmold in *Fabre's Book of Insects* by Jean-Henri Fabre, translated by Mrs. Rodolph Stawell (New York: Dodd, Mead. c. 1921).

Week Twenty-four:
The Sacred Beetle

"It is six or seven thousand years since the Sacred Beetle was first talked about. The peasant of ancient Egypt, as he watered his patch of onions in the spring, would see from time to time a fat black insect pass close by, hurriedly trundling a ball backwards. He would watch the queer rolling thing in amazement, as the peasant of Provence watches it to this day.

"The early Egyptians fancied that this ball was a symbol of the earth, and that all the scarab's actions were prompted by the movements of the heavenly bodies. So much knowledge of astronomy in a beetle seemed to them almost divine, and that is why he is called the Sacred Beetle. They also thought that the ball he rolled on the ground contained the egg, and that the young beetle came out of it. But as a matter of fact, it is simply his store of food.

"It is not at all nice food. For the work of this beetle is to scour the filth from the surface of the soil. The ball he rolls so carefully is made of his sweepings from the roads and fields.

"This is how he sets about it. The edge of his broad, flat head is notched with six teeth arranged in a semi-circle, like a sort of curved rake; and this he uses for digging and cutting up, for throwing aside the stuff he does not want and scraping together the food he chooses. His bow-shaped fore-legs are also useful tools, for they are very strong, and they, too, have five teeth on the outside. So if a vigorous effort be needed to remove some obstacle the Scarab makes use of his elbows, that is to say he flings his toothed legs to right and left, and clears a space with an energetic sweep. Then he collects armfuls of the stuff he has raked together, and pushes it beneath him, between the four hinder-legs. These are long and slender, especially the last pair, slightly bowed and finished with a sharp claw. The beetle then presses the stuff against his body with his hind-legs, curving it and spinning it round and round till it forms a perfect ball. In a moment a tiny pellet grows to the size of a walnut, and soon to that of an apple. I have seen some gluttons manufacture a ball as big as a man's fist.

"When the ball of provisions is ready it must be moved to a suitable place. The beetle begins the journey. He clasps the ball with his long hind-legs and walks with his fore-legs, moving backwards with his head down and his hind-quarters in the air. He pushes his load behind him by alternate thrusts to right and left. One would expect him to choose a level road, or at least a gentle incline. Not at all! Let him find himself near some steep slope, impossible to climb, and that is the very path the obstinate creature will attempt. The ball, that enormous burden, is painfully hoisted step by step, with infinite precautions, to a certain height, always backwards. Then by some rash movement all this toil is wasted: the ball rolls down, dragging the beetle with it. Once more the heights are climbed, and another fall is the result. Again and again the insect begins the ascent. The merest trifle ruins everything; a grass root may trip him up or a smooth bit of gravel make him slip, and down come ball and beetle, all mixed up together. Ten or twenty times he will start afresh, till at last he is successful, or else sees the hopelessness of his efforts and resigns himself to taking the level road.

"Sometimes the Scarab seems to enter into partnership with a friend. This is the way in which it usually happens. When the beetle's ball is ready he leaves the crowd of workers, pushing his prize backwards. A neighbour, whose own task is hardly begun, suddenly drops his work and runs to the moving ball, to lend a hand to the owner. His aid seems to be accepted willingly. But the newcomer is not really a partner: he is a robber. To make one's own ball needs hard work and patience; to steal one ready-made, or to invite oneself to a neighbour's dinner, is much easier. Some thieving beetles go to work craftily, others use violence.

"Sometimes a thief comes flying up, knocks over the owner of the ball, and perches himself on top of it. With his fore-legs crossed over his breast, ready to hit out, he awaits events. If the owner raises himself to seize his ball the robber gives him a blow that stretches him on his back. Then the owner gets up and shakes the ball till it begins rolling, and perhaps the thief falls off. A wrestling-match follows. The two beetles grapple with one another: their legs lock and unlock, their joints intertwine, their horny armour clashes and grates with the rasping sound of metal under a file. The one who is successful climbs to the top of the ball, and after two or three attempts to dislodge him the defeated Scarab goes off to make himself a new pellet. I have sometimes seen a third beetle appear, and rob the robber.

"But sometimes the thief bides his time and trusts to cunning. He pretends to help the victim to roll the food along, over sandy plains thick with thyme, over cart ruts and steep places, but he really does very little of the work, preferring to sit on the ball and do nothing. When a suitable place for a burrow is reached, the rightful owner begins to dig with his sharp-edged forehead and toothed legs, flinging armfuls of sand behind him, while the thief clings to the ball, shamming dead. The cave grows deeper and deeper, and the working Scarab disappears from view. Whenever he comes to the surface he glances at the ball, on which the other lies, demure and motionless, inspiring confidence. But as the absences of the owner become longer the thief seizes his chance, and hurriedly makes off with the ball, which he pushes behind him with the speed of a pickpocket afraid of being caught. If the owner catches him, as sometimes happens, he quickly changes his position, and seems to plead as an excuse that the pellet rolled down the slope, and he was only trying to stop it! And the two bring the ball back as though nothing had happened.

"If the thief has manages to get safely away, however, the owner can only resign himself to his loss, which he does with admirable fortitude.

He rubs his cheeks, sniffs the air, flies off, and begins his work all over again. I admire and envy his character.

"At last his provisions are safely stored. His burrow is a shallow hole about the size of a man's fist, dug in soft earth or sand, with a short passage to the surface, just wide enough to admit the ball. As soon as his food is rolled into this burrow the Scarab shuts himself in by stopping up the entrance with rubbish. The ball fills almost the whole room: the banquet rises from floor to ceiling. Only a narrow passage runs between it and the walls, and here sit the banqueters, two at most, very often only one. Here the Sacred Beetle feasts day and night, for a week or a fortnight at a time, without ceasing."

WORKS CITED

Fabre, Jean-Henri. *The Story-book of Science.* New York: The Century Co. 1917.

Stawell, Rodolph. *Fabre's Book of Insects: retold from Alexander Teixeira de Mattos' translation of Fabre's "Souvenirs entomologiques".* New York: Dodd, Mead and Company. 1921.

FOR FURTHER READING

Old World Echoes
New World Echoes
Ancient World Echoes
Uncle Paul's Science Stories
The Story of Rome Series
American Language Series
Scribblers to Scribes Curriculum
PreScripts
Fabre's Book of Insects